SEARCHING FOR DADDY IN THE DARK

Liquinita L. Callaham

Searching for Daddy in the Dark

634 NE Main Street #1263

Simpsonville, SC 29681

Text Copyright © 2019 by Liquinita L. Callaham

All rights reserved. No part of this book may be reproduced, scanned, or distributed in any printed or electronic form or by any means without prior written consent of the publisher, except for brief quotes used in reviews.

Please do not participate in or encourage piracy of copyrighted materials in violation of the author's rights. Purchase only authorized editions.

Library of Congress Control Number: 2019902938

ISBN 9780998026954

Printed in the United States

Dedication

To my babies Alexis Xzarria and Alysha Monee,' you are my most treasured gifts, greatest accomplishments, and the true loves of my heart. You are living proof that God can bring miracles out of any mess. You are not mistakes but a blessing, and being your mother is the joy of my life. You are special, wonderfully constructed by the mighty hands of God. My prayer for you is that you always be true to God, yourselves and others. Let God be your Father, Friend, and Guide all the days of your life. Know that God has a purpose for your lives and no matter where you go He will make sure you end up just where He ordained you to be, exactly when you are supposed to be there. Thank you for always believing in me, encouraging me and loving me without conditions or limitations. I know God made me just for you and He made you just for me. I love you oodles of noodles and bunches of crunches, past the moon into infinity.

Mommy

Mommy,

You are God's gift to me, all that I could have ever asked for, and more than I could have ever dreamed. Your love for me has been my saving grace and the most constant force in my life. Your strength is beyond my understanding but has carried me when I couldn't carry myself. Your smile brightens my soul and I am so grateful for who you are. You have always believed great things for me and it has been your faith in me that has made me a believer in myself. Thank you for giving your life to me so unselfishly and being the key contributing factor to my being as a mother. Our bond is unbreakable and our love is eternal!!!

Your heartbeat

Pops,

You are an answered prayer from the depths of my heart. Your love has been greater than any other that I have received from any man in my life. You are proof of God's love for me. Thank you for setting the bar high enough that I know never to settle for less. Thank you for providing the example of what to expect from a true man of God. Thank you for loving my mother in such a way that can never be duplicated. Thank you for being the man in my daughters' lives, showing them that love isn't always biological but a heart's choice. Your consistent unconditional love will live in my heart always. Thank you for filling the void in my heart and being the reason I have to search no more! I love you to infinity!

Your daughter,

Poo

In Loving Memory

Mr. David Warren, Sr.

January 12, 1948 – July 1, 2017

Introduction

Have you ever known that there was something you were supposed to do but you always found a reason to put it off until another day? Soon those days become weeks, weeks become months, and months turn into years without the execution of the purpose God placed in you. It's like carrying a baby for nine months and exceeding the due date. Discomfort sets in and all you want to do is give birth.

Our dreams are just like unborn babies inside of us. We hold on to them and nurture them until it's time to deliver, but sometimes we hold on too long. Maybe it's fear that holds us back. Or maybe thoughts of failure creep into our minds and take over. Or maybe we feel we are incompetent to be the mother of the dream God placed inside of us? For me, I just wanted to avoid the pain of labor and delivery. The gut-wrenching pain that I knew would come when I finally released the words into the atmosphere. Keeping silent meant that the world never had to know the guilt, pain and shame that have plagued my life for years. Keeping silent protected my children and spared my family from my pain. Keeping silent meant that I could continue to be who everyone thought I was. But keeping silent started to eat away at my mind and soul to where I couldn't find peace anywhere, not even with God. I felt unworthy and undeserving of the love that I desperately longed for. All I want is peace, and to gain that means I have to let the light shine into the darkness of my heart. The release of these words to come means I will no longer have to play the roles or hide behind the masks that have caused me to lose my identity. Truth will allow me to be who I am predestined to be, and that person has been lost for a very long time. As a matter of fact, this book is a journey to find out who she is and to let her live. I pray that my testimony can provide the same peace and healing for some other lost little girl trapped inside a woman, searching. But the truth is I'm writing this book primarily just for me. I need the healing. I need the peace. I need to let it all out because the weight has become too heavy to carry. I know that my Father in Heaven has forgiven me and in turn, I have forgiven many throughout the years. However, speaking my truth now will allow me to forgive myself and those who weren't so easy to forgive. Time to move forward! Time to give birth!

Disclaimer: This book was written from my perspective of events that I have experienced throughout my life. God has mended the broken places and healed my heart. I harbor no ill-will, resentment nor unforgiveness towards any parties involved.

Contents

		Page
"Sometimes I Call You Daddy"		8
Chapter 1	The Beginning	9
Chapter 2	Early Years	22
Chapter 3	Teddy	31
Chapter 4	Crushes	43
Chapter 5	Liberty & the Pursuit of Happiness	55
Chapter 6	Lesson Learned	67
Chapter 7	Growing Pains	84
Chapter 8	Test of Faith	100
Chapter 9	The Family Life	113
Chapter 10	Generations	131
Chapter 11	The Lost Years	138
Chapter 12	Lost	159
Chapter 13	Love Is…	182
Chapter 14	After Seven	214
Chapter 15	No Test, No Testimony	237
Chapter 16	Revelations	253
Acknowledgements		277

Sometimes I Call You Daddy

Sometimes I call him Daddy
Although that's not his name
I call him what I wish he was
But it doesn't change a thing
It doesn't make it so, nor does it make it real
The love I have in my heart for him
Is something he doesn't feel.

Sometimes I call him Daddy
In hopes that he'd reply
But my calls have gone unanswered
As years have passed us by.
Sometimes my heart still calls his name
I had to learn to let him go.
No more wishing for a daddy
That I will never know

Sometimes I call You Daddy
In Your Word you said I could
Never worry about you leaving
Because You promised You never would
Your love is unconditional, constant, and true
Everything that I've been searching for
I've always had in You.

Love your daughter,

Liquinita

Chapter One
The Beginning

Mommy has always told me that she loved me from the moment of conception. I found that hard to understand at first, but then she went on to explain to me how she felt about my father. She loved him with all her heart and soul and was happy to have a part of him growing inside of her. She says she remembers the very moment I was conceived, a summer night in June. My father told her to go home and take a douche; apparently, he wasn't as thrilled about the possibility of the new life he had implanted inside my mother. Lucky for me my mother opted not to follow my father's instructions.

My father was quite the ladies' man, or so I've been told. He was tall, dark and handsome...you know the type that women fall all over themselves for. He had a good job, car, and dressed very well. My mom was one of an unknown number of women that my father was allegedly involved with. But soon he settled down and married the mother of his first daughter, leaving my mother hurt and disappointed but not surprised. She knew based on her own personal reasons that she wouldn't or couldn't ever be his wife. Nevertheless, she was quite content to have the next best thing.

On March 16, 1975, I made my grand appearance and changed my mother's world forever.

Or at least that's what she tells me. Needless to say, my father wasn't a big part of my birth. Well to be honest he wasn't even there the day I was born. I came into this world at Self Memorial Hospital in Greenwood, SC welcomed by mother and grandmother. My mother says she hoped he would be there, but she knew that wasn't going to happen. She's often said that she wasn't going to force him to do what he should want to do on his own. Mommy had gotten herself prepared to take care of me without my father. My father was long gone although, he lived only twenty-five miles away with other family. I was all my mother had left of him. I could only imagine what it had to feel like to love someone with all your heart only to have that love unreturned. You would think that my father's absence would wax my mother's heart cold towards him. But my birth had the opposite effect. She loved him more because I was part of him, and so she carried that love deep inside her heart for years to come. But that's another story all by itself.

My mother was young when I came along. She had just graduated from high school and still lived at home with her mother and little sister. My papa also lived there...well when he and my grandmother were getting along. My mother said they fought often, physically! It was usually because of some other man, or in my Papa's case some other women. Nonetheless, neither of them was the "relationship type," but they kept trying.

Papa wasn't the father of my grandmother's

children; he was her on again off again long-term boyfriend. My mother said Papa was the closest thing she had to a father since her biological father wasn't a part of her life. Absentee fathers became a trend in my family. Anyway, Papa took care of the children and treated my mother and my auntie as his very own. So, he was the only grandfather I knew for quite some time.

The house we lived in was a tiny, white four-room shack that mother affectionately called "little house on the prairie." The house sat on a small plot of land with just enough room for a garden in the back. My papa raised pigs and once they were big enough, they were slaughtered for the meat. There were two rooms in the front of the house. One room was a combination living room and bedroom that contained a bed, dresser, couch and a wood-burning stove for heating. There was a plain-colored rug that covered the wooden floor in this room. A bedroom with a bed, dresser, and a wood-burning stove was next to the combination room. The family slept in these two rooms during the winter months to keep warm. My grandmother had her own room. My mother and auntie shared a bedroom, as well as the full-sized bed in it. When I came along, we were three to a bed. I slept tucked in next to my mother until I was a bit older. There was another bedroom in the back of the house containing the same furnishings of the second front room minus the wood-burning stove. My mother, auntie and I moved to this room during the summer months because it was the coolest in the house. And lastly was the kitchen which contained a stove, refrigerator and a table with four chairs. There was no sink because the house had no inside plumbing. All the rooms were of equal size.

The house did not have a bathroom or any running water. There was an outhouse in the backyard which my family used during the day. At night, pots were kept in the bedrooms and emptied each morning. There was a pan of water that was kept for washing hands. The family took baths in a large aluminum bathing basin. My grandmother kept a dish pan in the kitchen for washing dishes. There was water stored in case they needed but couldn't go get any. My mother and auntie were responsible for going to the top of the hill for water. They had to make sure that there was enough water for cooking, bathing and other necessities throughout the day. Mommy often talked about having to make the trip to the spigot several times a day. That was just one of the duties that my mother and auntie shared. They were responsible for keeping a clean house, gathering food from the garden, feeding the pigs that were later killed for the meat. They even had to chop wood for the heaters during the winter months. And this was life on the prairie for my family.

My mother has always been very strong and determined to have a better life than the one she was given. She once had dreams of joining the military and traveling the world, but that all changed when I came along. She had already starting working at Milliken, a local textile plant her senior year in high school. When I came along, her determination to provide a better life for herself and now for me intensified. She has always told me that she didn't have any other choice but to be strong to survive. She was also very adamant that I wouldn't have to endure the struggles she did. And she vowed that I would not be brought up around the violence she watched my grandmother endure.

The most important thing to my mother was being self-sufficient. She watched my grandmother struggle and depend on a man to provide for her. Mommy and my auntie made a pact in their early teenage years that after seeing my grandmother suffer, they would always be self-sufficient. No man would ever physically abuse them and they would never depend on a man to provide for them. My mother continued to work at Milliken, picking up more hours to provide for her family. My papa eventually moved out of the little house and my mother was the sole provider for our family. She had no idea what was lying ahead for her; she was only trying to make life just a little bit easier for all of us.

It was when my mother took me for my six-week checkup that her life would be forever changed. She took me to a quaint little office in McCormick where a husband and wife were both doctors. Actually, they were only one of two doctor's offices in McCormick during this time. During this appointment, my mother learned her perfect little girl was totally blind and had some severe problems with her heart. The only explanation the doctors offered for my condition was the diagnosis of German measles or more medically termed "Rubella". German measles is a viral infection distinctive by its red rash. It is a relatively mild disease which had an available vaccine. However, the disease can become more dangerous when the infection is passed from a mother to her unborn child. The infection can cause congenital rubella syndrome in developing babies, and that has devastating consequences. Babies infected with German measles before birth are at high risk for deformity of the eyes and heart, mental and growth retardation and numerous other serious health issues. My mother said her heart raced at the pending possibilities and she was consumed with fear for my life. She expected the doctors to offer her a glimmer of hope to save her precious daughter, but she received the exact opposite.

    The doctors' prognosis was extremely grim to say the least. They told my mother that I would probably die within my first year. And if I managed to survive, I would be developmentally delayed both mentally and physically. They told her it was highly unlikely that I would have a healthy and normal childhood because I would have so many health problems. They advised my mother that her best option was to spare herself the heartache of my death or trying to care for me and place me in a facility for disabled children. They told her that she was too young to take on such a huge responsibility. They warned her that the medical cost of caring for a child in my condition would be a tremendous financial strain. As if all of that wasn't enough, the doctors concluded that my mother could always have other children and she shouldn't burden herself with trying to care for me.

My mother told me how the doctors gave her every reason in the world not to keep me. She said they offered no hope at all. But my mother is the type of person who likes to defy the odds. They doctor told her I couldn't be saved and she vowed to prove them wrong. She promptly replied to the doctors that I was her child, she would never give me away, and they needed to refer her to someone who could help me.

Well I assume my mother's dedication to me sparked a flicker of hope in those doctors. Soon enough they offered several options for doctors, although at the time my mother had to do what was most practical and cost efficient for her. Mommy didn't have a car at this time, so she had to depend on family members to take us back and forth. Augusta, Georgia was the closest to McCormick that offered heart specialists. It was there at the Medical College of Georgia where our journey began.

The doctors at MCG (Medical College of Georgia) determined that I had an Atrial Septal Defect (ASD) and a Ventricular Septal Defect (VSD), more commonly referred to as holes in the heart. These malformations of the heart are the most common congenital heart diseases. These defects occur when there is a hole in the walls that separate the two upper chambers of the heart (ASD) and two lower chambers of the heart (VSD). If the holes are small, it's common for these to close on their own during infancy. However, that was not the case for me. The doctors informed my mother I would need to have open heart surgery to repair the holes in my heart. The doctors decided to give me time to grow and get stronger so I would have better odds at surviving the operation. I am assuming the urgency was not great because I didn't have the operation until I was nine months old. As you can imagine, that was of great relief to my mother. Of course, we had to make many trips to MCG for check-ups to make sure my heart was growing and developing properly. The doctors also had to keep a close eye on the holes to make sure they weren't getting too big and leaking too much blood. My mother said they were very careful to make sure that things didn't get worse.

During this time my mother relied heavily on family and friends to take us back and forth. She often talked about how everyone was so willing to help her with her baby girl. But the two most essential men in our lives were my Papa and great uncle Pap (I'm not sure what his real name was). They always made themselves available to take my mother to all of my doctor's appointments. Though there were many, they didn't mind one bit. As years passed I developed a very strong bond with them both, but you'll read more about them later.

After my issues with my heart were resolved, or at least for the time being, my mother's next focus was my eyes. I started going to the Greenwood Eye

Clinic under the care of Dr. Bobo. As a matter of fact, I was the youngest patient he'd had until that point. His diagnosis wasn't as grim as the country couple in McCormick had predicted. I wasn't completely blind and there was hope for restoration of my sight. Nevertheless, my condition was quite serious.

After careful examination, it was determined that I had Glaucoma and cataracts on my eyes. Glaucoma is a disease that causes fluid to build up in the front of the eye which creates a rise in eye pressure. This high pressure causes damage to the optic nerve that can eventually lead to blindness. I had the most common type, Primary Open Angle Glaucoma. This type is gradual, where the eye does not drain fluid properly, resulting in a rise in eye pressure over time. As a result of the rise in eye pressure, the optic nerve becomes damaged. Although this type of glaucoma is painless, it can and will most likely cause vision loss.

Cataracts are basically a clouding over the normally clear lens of the eye. The cataracts were assumed to be directly related to Rubella. Being that I was still an infant, the cataracts hadn't hardened. That made removing them easier. My very first of many eye surgeries was at six-month-old. The procedure was fairly simple; the doctors went into the eyes with a medicine dropper like needle and sucked out the milky cataracts from the lenses of my eyes. They also removed the fluid that was building in the front of the eye to prevent any further damage to my optic nerves.

And just like that, I was able to see. Dr. Bobo informed my mother that I needed to wear glasses to take some of the strain off my eyes and protect my vision. He also told her there would be some developing problems as I got older that would require additional surgeries, but it was too soon to tell what they would be. At that time, my mother was satisfied that she could see her baby and her baby could now see her.

The doctors at MCG monitored me very closely over the next few months. They wanted to make sure my heart was growing and developing as it should. But their greatest concern was that my heart wasn't overworking to meet the needs of my body. I was a rather small baby and there weren't many complications as I grew. However, the doctors decided it would be best to go in and close the holes before any major complications developed. So, at nine months old I had open heart surgery. My mother has talked to me countless times about this time in our lives. She has often told be about the love and support of her family. But there was never much mention of my father. I guess there was no point of mentioning someone who wasn't there. Each time we talked about this period in time, I often wondered what kind of father couldn't or wouldn't be there for his baby girl. I couldn't wrap my mind around the fact that he just couldn't be bothered to be there, especially at a time when my mother needed him most. She told me about how afraid she was of losing me. The operation was a risky one and I was quite small. The doctors told her of all the things that could go wrong. My mother told me once of the plan she made to end her life if I didn't survive. She said she couldn't live without me. Can you imagine loving someone that much? I hadn't even been in her life that long, but it didn't matter to her. She loved me fiercely ever since the moment she realized I was growing inside of her. Now that's some love for you right there.

The surgery went well and the doctors repaired the holes with no problem. However, there was an unexpected complication. There was a vein unattached to my heart, which needed to reattach for the heart to function properly. The reattachment process proved to be a bit tricky since I was small and the doctors worried about making sure it was secure. Nevertheless, it all worked out just fine. The operation was a success and I was now on the road to recovery. It appeared that everything was going well, which is not what the doctors had predicted at my six-week visit. Needless to say, my mother was overjoyed that I was doing so well.

I had to stay in the hospital for quite some time and of course my mother was right there. The doctors were closely monitoring the heart to make sure it was working as it should. They had to ensure the internal scarring from the surgery was healing properly and that there were no complications with any of my other organs. I was doing well, actually better than they had expected. My mother was also doing better; her determination to seek help for me turned into faith that everything would be okay. She had been there a long time and had developed friendships with other mothers who had children there. She had watched many mothers lose their children, which made her all the more grateful that I was doing so well.

There was an incident during my stay in the hospital where my mother had almost put her "plan" into action. It was during one of my feedings when she noticed I was breathing a little harder than usual. At first, she didn't think much of it. Later, all the color drained from my face and I turned a deep purple. I became limp in her arms and I was no longer breathing. My mother began screaming as loud and long as she could. The nurses came running in and took me away from her. They rushed me into the NICU where the doctors determined that my potassium had dropped significantly. Apparently, potassium is quite important to a person's survival. The doctors restored my breathing and replenished my potassium level. During this time, my mother was left waiting, not knowing what was happening to her baby. She contemplated all the possibilities, desperately afraid that she had just watched me die in her arms. She was determined not to live her life without me; therefore, her plan was to jump from the hospital roof. She gave no thought to those left behind but only to her daughter who she believed had left her. So many thoughts she experienced in what seemed like an eternity. The longer the doctors took, the more she considered her roof trip.

Finally, after what seemed like forever but was

actually only a few minutes, the doctors came and let her know I was going to be fine. She told me when I was older that was the single most terrifying moment of her life. "Life without you was not an option," she said.

After that last scare, things started to settled down. And soon I was released to go home. I wasn't on any medications or restrictions. However, I had to be on potassium for awhile in order to build my body up, which meant eating lots and lots of potassium-filled bananas. I'm not sure how long I had to eat bananas, but you best believe when I stopped I never started back. As you may have already guessed, I hate bananas with a passion.

I continued to grow and get stronger. I had a few more minor eye operations to stabilize my vision, but nothing too complicated. After that all was well in our little family living in our "little house on the prairie." During the next two years, my mother said my father would pop up every now and again. Sometimes he would stop by the house or just show up somewhere that he heard she would be. She never knew when he was coming or how long he was going to stay or if he would come back. She had no expectations for him. And before long, the visits stopped and my father was officially gone from my life before I ever got a chance to know he was there.

Chapter Two
Early Years

The next couple of years went by and I continued to do well. Of course, I would have regular checkups with the ophthalmologist and the cardiologist to monitor my condition but all in all I progressed very well. My mother often talked about how she had a time with me and my glasses. Needless to say, I didn't like them and threw them away every chance I got.

Mommy said there were times when we were out and she would be pushing me along in my stroller, then she would have to stop and check to see if I still had my glasses on. Most of those times, I didn't and she would have to turn around to retrace her steps to find them. She always found them and I always threw them away again. It became a little game we played, at least until I got used to wearing them. She said I was a smart even as a baby. And as I grew I advanced quickly. I talked early and was quite good at repeating what I heard. I was known around town as "the little girl with the old people sense." However, I was a late walker. The doctors told my mother it was because I had undergone so much and I would walk when I wanted to. It took some time, but one day while I was sitting in the kitchen I just stood up and walked away. I guess I grew tired of sitting.

My mother continued working to provide for

our family. My grandmother and my auntie took care of me while my mother worked. My mother worked a lot; sometimes she worked at night and other times she worked all day. Eventually, her hard worked paid off and she was able to get a house built. We left the "little house on the prairie" my mother and auntie grew up in and moved into our new home.

The house was bigger than the one we came from. It had three bedrooms, a bath and a half, a kitchen, a living room, and a few closets. There was even a smaller shed in the back yard for storage. There was a nice front porch surrounded by a gate. There was also a big yard in which I could run around. Other families lived near us. We lived in a neighborhood now, which was soon called the Bottom.

At the age of two or three, we received a new addition to our little family and it wasn't another child. My mother decided to get married, and due to my age my vote didn't count. My grandmother moved out of the house and got her own apartment. My auntie graduated from high school and went off to the military. So that left me, my mother and her new husband to become a family. Of course, I'm not clear on the details of this time because I was so young. All I know is what I have been told based on my mother's memory, which sometimes varies due to her seasoned years. I recall her telling me that soon after she was married she became pregnant with my sister. Unfortunately, I never got the chance to meet her because my mother miscarried. I am my mother's only living child. Now, let's fast forward to a time I do remember.

I was a very small child with what I thought to be an enormous head and even bigger glasses. I remember always hating my glasses because they made my eyes look like large floating saucers that didn't know which way they were going. My eyes had a mind of their own, and they were always wondering around. So even if I were looking directly at you, I appeared to be looking somewhere else. Even at a young age I knew that wasn't normal, and so did all the other kids. I was teased relentlessly from the time I started school. There wasn't another child like me in my class or even in the school. I was the only skinny, big-headed, thick glasses wearing child in McCormick. The name that sticks out the most is "four-eyes;" I heard it so much I actually started answering to it. I was called "blind" and "stupid" all the time. I was often asked futuristic questions, "What's for lunch next week?" or "Who is gonna win the game on Friday?" or "What questions are on the test?" because kids joked that my glasses were so thick I could see into the future. The kids played eye games with me by holding their fingers up and asking me how many I could see then they would quickly take one or two away. So when I answered, it would be wrong. They laughed hysterically until all the other kids joined in and the laughter turned into a loud roar. I just dropped my head and walked away; sometimes someone would stick their foot out so I would trip and fall. Sometimes I fell and other times I stumbled, but both were always attributed to my inability to see. I tried to think of something clever to say to retaliate. It never worked. The crazy thing is I continued to play along every time they did it to prove that I could see, but I always got it wrong. And each time I cried. I remember crying a lot, but never where they could see me. I couldn't let them know how much it hurt.

It was a little easier being at home. The neighborhood kids knew me and had become used my thick glasses. I had friends there and kids to play with without all the teasing. But every once in a while, (more often than I liked) I had an argument with one of them and they called me the same horrible names the school kids used. It hurt much more coming from someone that said they were my friend. My response was always the same. At home, I cried cry, stayed mad for a while, and then go right back to being their friend the next day. You would think I would have become immune to all the teasing after a while, but I never got used to it. It hurt more than I can put into words and I carried it with me. Just thinking of it now brings tears to my eyes. That pain became a part of me. The voices in my head became louder and my self-esteem dwindled almost down to nothing thereby shaping me into someone I didn't know. Maybe I will tell you about her later.

Of course, my mother fought my battles at home. Whenever I got into a fight with one of my neighbors, she made them apologize for calling me names or told them it wasn't nice to pick at people. She had this talk many times but it didn't help much.

She had no idea how bad the teasing was at school. Well at least not in full detail. I told her some things, but I kept most of the teasing I endured to myself. I wanted to be a big girl like she taught me, as strong as she was but I was nothing like her. She felt helpless because there was nothing she could do. She tried though, by telling me how pretty and smart I was. She poured herself into me, showering me with her love, affection and encouraging words. Sad to say but the negative words I heard from others were a thousand times louder than the positive words I heard from my mother. Each day at school was worse than the day before. Yes, there were some good days thrown in there and I had a few good friends, but it's funny how the bad stuff seems so much bigger.

  I was a good student. I soaked up everything I heard and learned like a sponge. I wanted to be good at something because in my young mind I concluded if I was good at something, my father would be proud of me. I wanted his approval even as a very young child. I missed him terribly. Now how you can miss someone you never knew or barely saw was beyond me. But what I did know is there was a hole in my heart where my father should be. It didn't help that all the other children in my neighborhood had a father. And although my mother got married and her new husband was my stepfather, it wasn't the same. I guess you wonder how I could feel so much at such a young age. Well, I'm not sure. The kids in my neighborhood didn't know that Teddy wasn't my biological father; everyone thought we were all a biological family like theirs so I didn't tell them any differently….at least not until many years later.

My Uncle Pap played a major role in my life as a little girl. I spent a lot of time with him during the summers. He was a constant in my life, someone that I trusted and could depend on. I will go so far as to say that he was the man in my life. He took care of me in ways that just came naturally to him but meant everything to me. He always greeted me with a hug, every single time he saw me, even if it was more than once in the same day. He told me how pretty I was even if I was all dirty and sweaty from playing outside in the summer heat. Those little things made me happy and I loved him so very deeply. Thinking back on him now brings tears to my eyes because I don't think he ever knew how much he meant to be. I never told him. I guess I figured I didn't have to because he wasn't much for sentiment. I just figured he had to know because I was sure he loved me.

Uncle Pap took my grandmother and me to the Fruit Stand almost every day during the summer. He came riding up the hill in his little blue car and blew the horn for us to come out. I ran outside to him and he got out to give me a big hug. I can see him so clearly standing there in his jean overalls (which seemed to be a bit too big), straw hat and black shoes…. he looked like a farmer but he wasn't. When we got to the store, he let me pick whatever I wanted and he picked a huge watermelon for us to eat. After we arrived home, he drank a raw egg, which he said kept him strong, and then he gutted the watermelon for us. We did this all summer long and I loved every minute. Uncle Pap was someone I could count on. Yea of course I had my mother, but he was a man that had been there since the beginning and he was still there.

Time flew by and I got older but never too old for my trips with Uncle Pap. One day I was waiting for him to come but he was late. It wasn't like him to be late because he always came around the same time on the days we went to the Fruit Stand, but this day he never came. Some family member went to his apartment to see where he was and that's where he was found dead. His death rocked my little world. I can still remember how sad I was and how I didn't understand why he left me. I just knew he would always be there and then he wasn't anymore. Losing Uncle Pap was the first loss I had ever experienced and though people have come and gone since then; his death is still the one that hurts the most.

I still had my Papa and he was just as special to me. Papa was a strong proud man who seemed to always have this serious look on his face. I can't remember him smiling much, but his eyes seemed to smile behind his glasses. He dressed like he was headed somewhere important with a button-down shirt, slacks and shiny, black shoes. Maybe he didn't always dress like that but that's the only image I can seem to pull up in my memory. He worked a lot, so I didn't get to see him that much. He came by as often as he could to take me for a ride in his big orange Thunderbird. I loved that car and I especially loved riding with him. I remember feeling important sitting in the front seat of that big car... There weren't all the car seat rules back then, so as little as I was I could still sit in the front and that made me happy.

Papa made me feel safe. I knew nothing was going to happen to me as long as he was around. He had a reputation around town as a man you didn't want to mess with. I knew he had a gun or two, but I never heard of him shooting anyone except for shooting grandmother in the leg. That was said to be accidental. I just knew that if I needed him he was coming, if I needed something he would get it, and whatever I wanted was mine. He was my grandfather and it didn't matter at all that there was no blood between us; he treated me like a princess. Sometimes we went to Augusta Georgia to see wrestling at the auditorium. I think it was something he enjoyed, but I couldn't care less. I just wanted to be with him, and of course get the mini cheeseburgers and fries from Krystal's afterward. I enjoyed being with him whether we were sitting outside on the porch, under the tree with his friends or just riding around in that big orange car of his. You might say he spoiled me because he was always giving me something.

My most precious gift from him was my very first Barbie Doll that he bought from the little store in town. It was a Peaches and Cream Barbie dressed in a long peach ruffles dress with a glittered top. I played with that doll all the time, and it was the one doll I wouldn't trade with my friends because my Papa gave it to me. That made it extra special.

I don't remember how or when but I know Papa started to change. He didn't come around as much. When I asked my mother, she told me he was sick. He had cancer and it hit him hard. We visited him since he could no longer come to us. I remember just sitting and watching him lie there in that huge bed that made him look so small. He slept a lot and I waited for him to wake so he could see I was there. Time seemed to stand still as I waited for him to get better, but he never did.

My papa died from cancer and I was left to live in a world without him. I felt not so important after he left, and why did I feel that at such a young age... I'm not sure. Maybe because he was the third man to leave me and I couldn't understand what I did to make this happen. Recalling it all now, I know I didn't do anything to make them die. But I sure felt like I did. This was just the beginning of the disappearing men in my life, either they died, left, or I pushed them away. Either way it happened: they were gone.

Chapter Three
Teddy

As I looked down at him lying helplessly in the hospital bed, I waited for some rushing flood of emotion. His face looked tired and worn as if he had carried the world on his shoulders for years and then finally let it fall. He looked defeated with no determination to fight anymore. His gray hair and beard won the battle against the black and took over. Heavy bags sat under his eyes and his face looked darker than its usual ebony brilliance. There were tubes all over hooked to one machine or the other. He lay motionless, not even aware that I was staring down at him. Surely there was going to be an explosion of tremendous pain now, and then my tears rushed down like a waterfall. I waited. Nothing. All I felt was sorrow and anger, way more anger than sorrow. I was sorry for all the time I loved him so much, sorry for all the years I believed in him, sorry for needing him…. depending on him, and sorry that he was never who I needed him to be. I was angry for the hurt he caused us, angry for being sorry, so angry because he had the chance to be my daddy and failed. More than anything, I was angry because there was a part of me still screaming, after all these years, for him to love me and wake up and be my father. Looking down at him now, I didn't see the broken man who needed me to be there. All I saw was the man who caused me so much pain. And the memories overtook me, then uncontrollable tears.

My mother and I came home from church one night to find Teddy outside waiting. He was angry and I guess he had been drinking. For some reason, he believed my mother was not being truthful about where she really was. He began screaming at her with profanities and calling her foul names. She screamed back in defense as I stood there watching. I remember not understanding what was going on or why and being really scared. Even then I knew this wasn't normal behavior because my friend's parents didn't act like this. Suddenly my mother grabbed my tricycle and flung it at him. She missed. He quickly shrunk back in shock and went into the house. And just like that it was over. My mother took my hand and we followed him into the house. This was my very first memory of Teddy and the first of a childhood of drunken rants, arguing, fighting and what I know now to be a cycle of dysfunction.

Teddy was tall and dark. I guess you could say he was handsome if that's what you liked. My mother certainly did. He had big curly hair that I'm sure wasn't naturally that way. His face was round, dark and shiny. He had the smoothest, darkest, most flawless skin that I had ever seen on a man with his complexion. His eyes were a sparkling white with a dark brown circle in the center. I think his best feature was his pretty, white straight teeth that sat under a thick, black mustache. Those teeth were immaculate; consequently, that gave him a beautiful smile. He wasn't a fat sloppy, kind of guy; he was solid like a big, black brick wall. This was a wall built to protect those inside it and keep all dangers away. I loved him so much, but I'm not even sure why. He certainly didn't do anything to earn it. It just came naturally to me, no matter what he did or what anyone told me, I loved him unconditionally largely because I desperately needed him to love me back.

  Teddy absolutely adored my mother. He worshipped the ground she walked on. He was constantly telling her how beautiful she was and how much he loved her. I saw him watching her sometimes as she moved around the house. He looked at her in pure adoration like she was the only woman alive. Everyone knew how much he loved her maybe because he told anyone who would listen. And as far as I knew, she loved him the same way. It didn't take me long to realize that he didn't love me the way he loved her. As a matter of fact, looking back on it, I am sure he didn't love me at all. But at that time, I didn't care because I was determined to make him love me. This was a chance for me to have the father I so desperately longed for. I figured that if I could show him I was a good little girl, that it would be easy for him to love me. I did everything my childlike mind could think of. I begged for his attention, wanting to do what he did and go with him wherever he went. Most of the time, he told me no but that didn't keep me from asking time and time again. He loved to watch wrestling, and although I wasn't very fond of it after Papa died, I sat and watched just to be with him. Whatever he asked me to do for him I did to show him that I loved him. I believed whatever he told me, even though he lied all the time. I had absolute faith in him, even though all his actions showed me that was not a good idea. I wanted him to be a good man so he would be a good father to me. But the truth is he wasn't interested in being my father. He only wanted my mother, and I was just extra baggage.

Living in the house with Mommy and Teddy was a rollercoaster ride. There were extreme highs and devastating lows. And the highs were amazing; we appeared to be a loving happy family. However, I can't seem to remember many times like that. And where there was a high, a low was sure to follow but I never knew when or how low we would go. The lows had a trigger, which was usually alcohol. Teddy was much more than a social drinker; he was a drunk. Thinking back, I can't ever remember him drinking at home. He always went out and got with his friends and drank. Then he came and we never knew what to expect.

My mother was usually the target of Teddy's alcoholic rage. When he was drunk, he was paranoid. And in this paranoia, he always thought my mother was being unfaithful. I guess somewhere between working ten hours and swinging shifts, she managed to meet another man that treated her better than he did. The funny thing is I never saw this mystery man that Teddy was sure existed somewhere. But nevertheless, he had convinced himself this man was out there plotting to take her away from him. He yelled, called her "bitch" and "whore." Sometimes, he got in her face as if to threaten her or make her afraid. But she was never afraid of him. My mother never backed down from Teddy, not one time. She fired angry words back at him threatening to hurt him if he didn't back off. Although, he never admitted it, he was more afraid of my mother than he thought she was of him. This went on for awhile until Teddy got tired and finally passed out into a drunken hibernation. He woke up a few hours later with no recollection of the argument between him and my mother. When my mother told him, he said he was sorry and begged for forgiveness. He always cried and pleaded with mommy not to leave him, promising to never drink again. Of course, he never kept his promise and so the cycle continued: drinking, arguing and then apologizing.

My mother was fierce. I have never seen her back down from anyone. She was the strongest woman I knew and still is. But my mother had a temper, one of which you wouldn't think lived in a woman so beautiful. When she got angry, there was no way to predict her reaction. When the tears started to roll from her eye, that was fair warning to whoever was in her path to get out of the way. If she were pushed in a corner, she would come out swinging. And she swung at Teddy a lot. Sometimes when Teddy came home in one of his drunken rages, she was ready for him. I've seen things fly off the wall, from the fridge or the closet, objects she'd grab and throw in the air aiming for Teddy's head, usually missing it by just an inch or two. Every time, his eyes grew bigger and wider in shock, but mostly in fear. Then, he backed down from all is ranting, cursing, and name calling. And so, the cycle began again.

Once when I was in elementary school, I had a friend come spend the night. It just so happened to be one of the Fridays Teddy didn't come home from work. After playing all afternoon and a good bit of the night, my friend and I went to bed. We were awakened by a loud crash; the sound came from my parent's room. I don't remember what was knocked over that night, but I do remember the screaming and yelling that followed. Teddy came home drunk again and he was ranting about something. Then the arguing started. I remember it being so bad that my friend and I were both crying. She was so scared and wanted to go home.

My mother came in and took us out of the room trying to calm us down. Teddy followed her screaming at her and falling over things. She was yelling back at him to stop acting up and leave her alone. He didn't. He picked himself up and kept coming for her. He pushed her hard and she pushed him back. My friend and I cried harder. This was the first time I saw him get physical with my mother. We ended up outside on the porch that night. My mother was trying to protect us from him. I don't remember being afraid of him at all, just upset because this was happening. It took quite a while for Teddy to settle down and go to bed. But the damage was already done.

My friend was terrified and that Monday at school she told everyone about my drunken father and how scared she was. Now my secret was out, everybody knew I had an alcoholic father. And as embarrassed as I was, I remember trying to defend him. He was my daddy, I loved him, and so I protected him. Needless to say, I didn't have too many sleepovers after that.

Sometimes my mother wasn't there when Teddy came home. These were the times that I had to deal with him by myself. I was older and learned what to do by watching my mother. Normally, he came in looking for my mother. Once he realized she wasn't there, he started with the questions. Where is she? How long has she been gone? Who did she go with? When will she be back? I answered the questions exactly as she told me to because I didn't want him to get upset; I always expected him to get upset but he never did. I observed the tears and long rants about how much he loved my mother and how he didn't want to lose her.....blah, blah, blah. Then midsentence, he would fall off to sleep. I tried to move him from the couch before my mother came home (she got mad when he passed out on her living room couch) but he was too heavy and sometimes I couldn't get him up. Other times, I managed to get him up and he staggered into the bedroom and pass out across the bed. There were also times when he didn't rant, he just went to the bedroom and passed out on the bed. These were the times I hated the most. I always checked on him to make sure he made it to the room because sometimes he didn't. I found him there stripped down to his tighty whities sprawled across the bed. I didn't think a daughter should see her father this way but I did, more times than I can count. I hated it. I tried to cover him up and sometimes he fought me, which made it extra hard. Other times he was in a drunken slumber so I covered him without a problem.

Then there were also the times that Teddy didn't make it to the bed. Maybe he made it to the hall in front of the room, to the bathroom next to the room, or even worse, my room instead of his on. Sometimes he was clothed and sometimes not. These times I had to help him up and guide him to the room. It was in these moments that he told me he loved me. "Daddy loves you PooPoo" he said right before closing his eyes into drunken sleep.

Those times meant so much because in my mind his words were true. Drunken men tell no tales they say. Who wants a drunken, "I love you?" I sure didn't, but I held onto it anyway because maybe there was a chance he did love me...maybe.

Teddy was a liar. I'm not trying to be mean but it's true. He lied all the time with such ease, most times for no reason at all. I knew this about him and accepted it as fact, but I convinced myself that he never lied to me. If he told me he wasn't going to drink again, I believed him until he got drunk again. If he told me we were going somewhere together, I believed him until we didn't. If he told me he was going to give me this or that, I believed him until he didn't. The list goes on and on, yet I continued to trust him because one of those times wouldn't be a lie. I needed Teddy to come through for me; he was the only man I had left. I poured all my faith and hope into him. He was my daddy.

As time passed things didn't improve much. The only difference was that I was more aware of what was going on. My mother couldn't hide it from me as she tried to in the past. Teddy never slowed down on his drinking. And soon drinking, wasn't his only problem, he started using drugs, too. I'm not sure what kind: I never asked and my mother didn't tell me. I just knew that there was a shift in his behavior. He was different. I became more afraid of him. I never knew what he might do. He thought nothing could touch him when he was using. The arguing got worse, so much so that I didn't like being at home but I never wanted to leave my mother alone with him. I was afraid that one day he would follow through on one of his drunken threats that were now intensified with drugs. He never hurt her physically; nevertheless, he hurt her badly. I never realized how much until many years later.

With the drugs and alcohol also came more lies, but now the lies started to affect our house. Every Friday evening Teddy brought his check home to my mother so she could pay the bills and get groceries; however, sometimes the money wouldn't make it home. He would tell my mother he was robbed or he lost his check. Other times he told her he didn't get paid. And then there were the times when he was supposed to leave the money on the dresser and it would be short. When Mommy asked him about it, he swore he gave it all to her but he hadn't. So, there were times when the lights were turned off or mommy had to wait to get food and pay other bills. She got so mad and usually an argument ensued. My mother cried and these were the times I hated the most. I didn't like to see her cry. Nevertheless, she pulled it together and came up with the money somehow. No matter how bad things got, she always made sure I had everything I needed and most of what I wanted with or without Teddy's help.

Along with the drinking, drugs, lies, and lost money came the other women. This was the part I really never understood. Teddy worshipped my mother and he loved her so much. So why did he cheat? Why did he do the one thing he was always accused her of doing? I don't know. She was a good wife. She cooked every day (well almost every day), kept the house clean, clothes washed and taught me to do the same. She put up with a lot from him and stayed with him when most women would have left. Why didn't she just leave? I don't know that either. These women would call to our house for him. All she would say is, "Tell your women to quit calling my house." He would always say, "What women? You know I don't want nobody but you sweetheart." But of course, he was lying. People told my mother about the other women. There were a few times my mother even talked to the women Teddy was messing around with. But still she stayed and still he drank, lied, did drugs, brought home no money, and cheated. It wasn't until I left for college that she left him.

There were some good times thrown in the mix. These were the highs. We went places together and had the best time. My mother was happy and Teddy was smiling. There was hand-holding and other displays of affection. I was happy. We were a normal, happy family and the drunken monster was gone at least for a little while. I so loved these times. My mother had gotten saved and things started to change in our house. We went to church more, although I was already attending with the neighbors. Even Teddy came sometimes and he got saved too, quite a few times actually. I think he thought this is what he needed to do in order to keep my mother. And I guess it didn't stick, that's why he felt the need to do it over and over again. However, my mother never believed him and she was right not to, but I did. It was in these times that he stopped drinking. He and I did things together. One of my favorite memories with him is watching *The Wizard of Oz*. His favorite character was the cowardly lion. He laughed so hard at him and then mocked him saying, "Put em up, Put em up. I'll fight you with both fists behind my back." I laughed so hard until tears rolled down my checks. He laugh some more and he would say it again. I would laugh harder than the first time. It was great. I'm sure there were other happy memories mixed in there somewhere, but this is one that has stayed with me throughout my life. It is this single

memory that told me in that moment I was his daughter, he was my daddy, and he loved me. If only for the moment.

Chapter Four
Crushes

I never really felt good enough. Looking back now I know it was because I wasn't being authentic. See, I was constantly changing, becoming whoever, someone wanted me to be in order to be accepted. I did things that I didn't necessarily want to do but did so I could fit in. For example, I had a friend who stopped talking to another friend of mine for whatever reason. She told me if I was going to be her friend I had to stop talking to her too, so I did! I knew it was wrong but I did it anyway. Why? I don't even know! That's just one of many examples of my stupidity. I can't remember anything real about me back then, except for my heart. My heart was pure and all I ever desperately wanted was to belong. But I went about it all the wrong way. I was sneaky and I lied sometimes for no reason at all. I made up stories that I thought would make me more likable. I wasn't good at it at all. So, if there was some drama going on, you better believe I was in the midst of it somehow. I was overly dramatic, highly expressive of whatever I was feeling. I just wanted someone to pay attention to me, like really see me! I was constantly searching for something or someone to hold on to. There was no way anyone could give me what I needed because I didn't know quite what I needed myself.

It was middle school when I noticed him. There wasn't anything spectacular about him. He wasn't the most popular guy at school. As a matter of fact, he wasn't popular at all. He wasn't drop dead gorgeous nor did he have the greatest body. He wasn't athletic or part of a lot of extracurricular activities if any. He was just an ordinary guy, okay maybe, not even that ordinary. He was different. No matter what he wasn't, he was something special to me. And I don't even know why but I was drawn to him. I don't remember how or when it happened but I fell for him as hard as a ton on of bricks. I don't remember liking him, it seemed like I loved him instantly. But of course, he didn't give me the time of day, at least not at first. Everyone at school knew I had a crush on him and teased us both relentlessly. He didn't like that at all and sometimes he called me names just to prove to the other kids that he didn't like me. You would think this would change the way I felt about him. Nope, it didn't. The teasing didn't bother me because I liked being called his girlfriend, even if it wasn't true.

I tried everything to get his attention but I wasn't the type of girl he wanted. Actually, I wasn't the type of girl anyone wanted, which I thought would give him incentive to date me because there weren't girls knocking down his door either. He finally noticed me; he just didn't let anyone else notice that he did. Time passed and I finally got my first kiss. It was AMAZING, probably because I had nothing to compare it to. Nonetheless that one kiss sent me spinning and we were already married with 2.5 children in my head. I just wanted to be with him and so when I could, I would. He would come over sometimes after school and we would fool around. I liked feeling him close to me, touching me, and kissing me. He was my first everything, well almost everything because I was a bit of a tease. There was no way I was going to have sex. But I did do other big girl things that left my body all tingly inside. However, when we got to school the next day, he acted as if he didn't know me.

This went on for quite some time. We were off again on again but never officially a couple. Although I do remember this one time he gave me a valentine at school. Typical me, I took this to mean that this was it, he was letting the world know that I was his girl...wrong!!! Maybe it was so I would keep letting him come over and have make out sessions. I did. Either way he was all over me at my house and barely acknowledged me at school. I honestly can't blame him because I allowed him to treat me this way. I was just so desperately wanted the attention, even if no one else could see. I wanted him to want me and he did, like most guys wanted girls in that way. It didn't matter because I still loved him. For years, I loved him so much that I didn't care how he treated me. I filled my diary with pages of my love for him, then my hate for him, and finally my hope that he would one day love me, too. He never did.

This was the start of guys rejecting me, hurting me, and me telling myself that if I loved them enough that they would love me back. Kind of sounds familiar, huh? Well, it should because I started this cycle long before the crushes began and it would continue and worsen as time passed by. Let me be clear, I take full responsibility for a lot of things that have happened to me. I put myself in some messed up situations on a search for what was missing. All I wanted was for someone to love me. Correction, all I wanted was to be loved and accepted by a man…any man. I didn't go searching for it. But my heart just seemed to latch on to boys or men that I thought could give me what I needed.

Throughout the rest of my middle school years and on to high school I had quite a few crushes. I was the kind of girl who fell fast and hard. And when I decided I liked someone, I was devoted to my crush whether he knew it or not. This type of blind devotion got me in trouble sometimes and caused me to compromise myself in ways that no girl should have to. Not for the temporary attention of some guy. I wasn't the type of girl that boys wanted to date but the type that they wanted to fool around with behind closed doors. Maybe I appeared way too easy. And I will admit I could be easy. I never did anything I didn't want to do, but there were plenty of things I shouldn't have done. There was a lot of kissing and fondling. My body was starting to feel things that it enjoyed and craved more of. There were way too many close calls with almost sex to mention. But then again, I vowed not to have sex before I graduated high school and I didn't. Boy was I a tease, but I always let the boy know up front that I wasn't having sex. However, many tried to change my mind. And I must admit I liked for them to try. I liked having a guy desiring something from me that he could only have IF I decided to give it. That kind of power gave me a sense of importance and worth and I used it to my advantage. If my mother had any idea of some of the things that I did….well, let's just keep that between us. I was from one guy to another searching for something that I never found. (Okay, let's pause right here for a second, there weren't a whole slew of guys but there were enough to be too many. Unpause.)

    I started reaching out to my father a lot. I called his house just to hear his voice, then I hung up. He rarely ever answered anyway. Sometimes I found the courage to ask for him, but I was always denied. There was no caller ID back then, so no one ever knew it was me but I expected them to know. By then, I knew I had brothers and a sister but they knew nothing about me. Anger started to fester in my heart and I tried to hate them all, but I couldn't. I still wanted to know my father and now my siblings. At one point, I think I became obsessed with trying to contact him. Somehow, I guess my father figured out it was me calling and my mother found out. She told me to stop calling and so I did, for a while at least. You would think I was crushing on my father the way I had romanticized him in my head. I couldn't wait to meet him and unexpectedly, I finally did. I was at my mother's job one day when one of her friends called me over and said "This is your father." We both stood there staring at each other, he said, "Hello," and then walked away. I just stood there with this huge pain in my chest and I decided I wasn't going to love him anymore. But that didn't last long!

    I had a boyfriend once, well kind of but not really. We were good friends and of course I was crushing on him. But he was also crushing on me. No one understood why I liked him, neither did I but I did. He was a cutie, at least I thought so. He was full of himself and I was attracted to that kind of confidence. We talked on the phone, hung out together and flirted with one another. I thought this was it. Then he started to come visit me and he met some of my friends. All of a sudden, I was just a friend as he tried to date a few of my friends. Oh, but when there was no one else around he wanted to be all touchy feely. And stupid me let him touch and feel wherever he liked. Some attention is better than none, right? At least I thought so. Needless to say, we never made it official. I soon wised up and put an end to all the fooling around. We remained friends, good friends. And that's mainly because I'm great at holding on to those I should let go.

    I remember having a crush on this one guy who wouldn't even give me the time of day. As a matter of fact, he was interested in my cousin. But I didn't care; I was young and selfish. I wanted him and I came up with a plan to get him. See, he lived in another state and all I had to do was convince my mother to let me go there for the summer. I knew my cousin's parents wouldn't let her go but my mother would because we had family there. So, I went. At first, he didn't pay me any attention as he continued to talk to my cousin. But eventually, we started spending more time together and he changed his mind. It was kind of easy because I was there and she wasn't. I know what you're thinking, and yes, I did feel badly. But apparently not too bad. It was something about him that went far beyond his cuteness. He was intense, like real mature for his age and very intelligent. We became fairly close. We talked all the time; sometimes we stayed up all night just talking. We started messing around a little, kissing, hugging, and touching. I thought I was a big little girl, sneaking around with this guy. It was exciting coming so close to sex but never quite getting there. I was much too young to be having sex, but he didn't think so.

    I started to realize he didn't want a girlfriend, he just wanted sex. He kept trying to get me to change my mind but I stayed firm. He started to show me another side of him; he had a horrible temper. He would get so mad whenever I didn't do what he wanted. He yelled and screamed, throwing things, and calling me all sorts of names. There were times when he even tried to force himself on me and I had to fight him off. Once, I locked myself in the bathroom to get away from him. Another time, I ran outside so he wouldn't get me. I was y quite terrified of him, I never knew what trigger set him off. But there were other times when he was kind and gentle, and that's the guy I was falling for. He apologized for losing his temper and I always forgive him. This cycle happened again, over and over, and I continued to forgive him. For some reason, I was drawn to him. His parents treated him terribly, so, I just wanted to be there for him. So, I let him do whatever he wanted to do with me, except sex which he took as me rejecting him. All of it was very confusing to me. I didn't understand how one minute he loved me and the next he acted as if I was his worst enemy. He was a great guy, until he wasn't. I didn't tell anyone what was happening. I just let it happen. I loved him. I'm not sure why but I truly did. Eventually, I had to leave but his hold over me lasted a long time after I was gone.

Then there was Champ. There was nothing spectacular about this one either. He was just kind and somewhat popular. He was an ordinary run-of-the-mill sort of guy who just happened to have a pretty good personality and great generosity. He reminded me a lot of myself. Who ever knew a hotdog could alter someone's life in such a drastic way. Yea, a hotdog. See I was hungry, as I often am so he bought me a hotdog and there blossomed a wonderful relationship. I didn't like him, and by that, I mean in the way a girl likes a guy. I just thought he was a nice guy. While by this time in my high school social relations I had some friends that were guys, he was set apart from the rest. Over time we got to know each other and became fast friends. We talked on the phone almost every day. We talked about all sorts of things and I started to feel comfortable enough to let him get close to me. Most importantly he never once teased me or called me names. We were friends at home and at school. He looked out for me. He stood up for me. And when I needed him, he was usually there. And boy was I needy. I made it a point to be there for him as well, a little give and take to keep things balanced. He called me on my crap and yes, I could be quite crappy at times. He never treated me differently than he treated any of his other friends.

    We became great friends. I even went so far as to say best friends. We had a lot of things in common. We were both the only child being raised primarily by our mothers. We were both middle class socialites at school. And we both had fathers who had no interest in being a part of our lives. He was my constant, someone I could depend on and although we didn't always agree, our friendship remained solid. It was through him that I made other friends and began to hang out a little. My mom trusted him with me, which is something she didn't do easily or often. He was older than me, so of course he got his license first. I never got mine but that didn't keep me from taking the car for a little spin every now and then. But that's another story for another book. Anyway, my mother allowed him to drive her car to take me places sometimes. So, by this time he was in well with the family. He was the only guy my mother let come to the house when she wasn't home, the only one I could talk to late on the phone, and the only one that was truly a significant part of my life. He was the kind of guy that your parents wanted you to bring home. I was glad to have him around.

I was very territorial when it came to him. He was the only guy who had come into my life and stayed awhile. I didn't want to lose him. Pointless to say but I will anyway, I loved him very much. Of course, he had no idea. Besides, I wasn't the type of girl he went after anyway. Thinking back on it, I don't think he rejected me as much as he just liked what he liked. I didn't see it that way then. I didn't understand why he couldn't see how much I loved him. I was the one who was always there for him. I was the one who was there when he was rejected by the girls he went after. I was the one who did anything for him. But I wasn't the one he chose. I stood by as he dated girl after girl, some of whom were my friends. I even went so far as to set him up with girls I knew he liked or who liked him. I spoke on his behalf; you know talked him up to these girls. I just tried to stay in the friend zone. He saw me as his little sister, so I stayed in my place.

But there were others who could see my feelings for him no matter how hard I tried to hide them. And I did try very hard. I didn't want to do anything to ruin our relationship. These feelings I was having started to create distance between us. He had already made it perfectly clear to anyone who asked that we were just friends and it would never be anything more. He tried his best not to do anything to encourage my feelings or give me the wrong message. So, we didn't talk as much or spend as much time together, especially when he had a girlfriend. I took this change in behavior as rejection and it hurt me more than I can express. I didn't understand why my love wasn't enough for him. It was only a reminder of all the other times I loved to no avail. It must have been a tough spot for him to be in having his best friend loving him, and everyone trying to force something that was never meant to be. At the time, I didn't care. I wanted what I wanted, so I told him how I felt...well at least I tried to. But he didn't love me in that way. However, he did love me. Not in the way a boy loves a girl, but in that protective big brother loves an annoying little sister kind of way. It wasn't the way I wanted but exactly what I needed, more than I knew at the time. Even through all the craziness I put him through he never gave up on me. He stayed constant. He protected my heart in a way that no one else had ever done before. He was the real deal and I couldn't understand why other girls didn't see what I saw. It didn't matter because girls came and went in his life, but I remained. That had to mean something, right? Well of course it did.

I didn't understand the gift that God had given me in my relationship with him. I was too busy trying to turn it into something it wasn't meant to be. I just wanted love, real and true love and I didn't realize that God gave me exactly what I asked for, but it took him leaving for me to figure that out. After he was gone I missed him terribly and I didn't think I would ever get past the pain of his absence. He called as often as he could and he wrote letters to keep in touch. He was still there! It was in his absence that I appreciated what he meant to me. My love for him was so great, my heart didn't know what to do with all of it. It was an unconditional lifetime kind of love. He was truly my brother in every sense of the word. He had been there when I needed him, corrected me when I was out of line (which was a lot), listened to, protected me, and remained my very best friend. What more could I have asked for? What I felt for him was gratefulness because he stood by me through all my mess, and I had a heap of mess. All I wanted was for him to be there and he was. I wanted him to choose me and he did. I wanted him to love me and he did in a way that my father never did. He was able to see what I couldn't, which was the love and friendship we had developed would stand the tests of time…and it did!

Chapter Five
Liberty and the Pursuit of Happiness

I graduated high school without ever having a date, a boyfriend or falling in love. Well except for that one time in middle school but you saw how that played out. It didn't matter because I had survived so much. I was diagnosed with Glaucoma but I was still able to see. I just couldn't drive…. legally anyway. When I was seventeen the doctors told my mom I had to have another open-heart surgery. This time I was old enough to be terrified even though she wasn't; I was sure I was going to die. My mom gave me a party right before I went in the hospital. Now many people would have taken this as a celebration, well not me. I saw it as a death party, a last time to see all the people I loved before I went to heaven. Dramatic huh, well that was me, Ms. Drama…a death party…really mommy? Oh well, I didn't die. Instead I was headed to college, which offered new opportunities to do all the things I didn't do in high school. My cousin and I were both accepted to school in Columbia, SC and we were going to be roommates. Then one phone call changed everything.

It was midsummer when Spike called asking me to consider coming to college in Virginia. Of course, I said, "No," but that didn't keep him from calling every day that week. He offered me a full ride, room and board included, if I would change my plans and come there. By this time, we had talked a lot and yet again I was drawn to another guy. Did I want to be that far from home? No! Would I really renege on my plans with my favorite cousin? Of course not, but I did. And it was not because this was such a great opportunity. It was not because this was such a great school and I could go for free. Nope! It was because he was a junior, had a great voice, was cute, and he was interested in me. So, it was Virginia here I come! Of course, my mother didn't know my true motives; she was just happy that I was going to school there. Sorry, Mommy!

This would be my first time away from home. Although I didn't want to leave my mother; I felt this is something I needed to do. Why? I don't know. I would like to think that my choice wasn't all about Spike, but he did have a great impact on my decision. My mother and I were extremely close by the time I left for college. Her love for me was greater than any love I had ever known. And of course, I loved her too, and would miss her terribly. But there was a part of me that needed to know what life was like without her everyday presence. I wanted a chance to experience some things on my own, make my own choices and yes make some mistakes. I was ready to try something new and different. I was ready to start over somewhere new. So, I attended Liberty University in Lynchburg, Virginia.

I cried when my mother dropped me off at school. I thought I was ready to be without her but clearly, I was mistaken. And there we were both crying in the hallway of my dorm. I didn't want her to leave me there. I was terrified. She soon left and she later told me she cried all the way home. For six hours, she cried. We had never been apart in my eighteen years of life. Yea, I had a few sleepovers, but I was never so far that she couldn't get to me quickly. Now we were separated by two states and neither one of us knew it would hurt this much. I dried my face and went in to get acquainted with my roommates. One of them was from Pennsylvania and the other was from New York. Both seemed very nice and I had no doubt that we would get along great. And for the most part, we did. I got there too late so I missed the bottom bunk. I was very disappointed about that but I tried not to let it show. I took the top bunk over one of my roommates and unpacked most of my things before I headed out to finally meet Spike in person.

    There was a large crowd of people gathered in the courtyard. The school gave a welcome gathering for the freshman each year. The upperclassman would also be there as a part of the welcoming committee, so I was sure Spike was there somewhere. I combed the crowd searching for him. I was so excited and had completely forgotten about how scared I was. I figured I had one up on everyone else there because I came there already having a friend, an upper classman friend. I eventually hooked up with my roommates, but I continued to look for Spike. I didn't let them know that I was looking for anyone. As a matter of fact, I didn't tell them about Spike at all. I never found him that day, but I knew we would see each other soon.

It was a few days later when I saw Spike on campus. He walked up and discreetly said, "Hello." He was looking around a lot and I wasn't sure why. He asked for my number, I gave it to him, and he quickly walked away. I had a chance to get a good look at him and he looked nothing at all like the picture I had received earlier that summer. Don't get me wrong, he wasn't a bad looking guy. He just wasn't drop dead gorgeous; you know the kind you would change your college plans for. He was dressed in jeans, a t-shirt, and a baseball cap, which hid his face a little. He wore glasses and spoke very proper. I could tell in that moment he was intelligent. I can now assume he was not too impressed with my appearance, given his behavior. Nevertheless, I answered the phone when he called later that night. We talked for a while, then he asked me to meet him downstairs. By this time, my roommates and I had established a system where we always let at least one roommate know where we were just in case anything happened. If anything ever happened to me, no one would have known because I never told anyone when I was meeting Spike. Thinking back on it, I'm not sure why I didn't say anything.

Spike and I started to hang out a lot. We went out to eat, and I paid the majority of the time. We visited the park and talked. And sometimes, we just sat in his car but never on campus. I never met any of his friends and he never met any of mine. He never came to my dorm, nor did I go to his. No one ever saw us together in public. And if we happened to be in public and saw one another, we never said a word to each other. This is how he wanted it. No one could know about me and I agreed like a dummy. Whenever he called to the room for me, I told my roommates he was just a guy I knew. I never offered up any more information than that. Spike had a very dominant personality and I easily fell in line. So usually when he asked for something I gave it, when he told me to do something I did. This was largely in part to wanting to keep him happy so he would stay with me. For some crazy reason, I thought I was something special because he chose me.

Soon we started meeting in secluded place where we couldn't be found for our make out sessions. I never had a boyfriend before, so I didn't know how this part of the relationship was supposed to go. I was always where he told me to be, which was usually a dark room somewhere. We never turned on the lights; we would just find one another in the dark and go at it, kissing, touching and grinding in a way that had to be passion. It was like we were starving for this time together and couldn't get enough of each other. The kisses were hot and heavy, deep and full of lust. I could feel his hands roaming over my body, touching my hidden place. I felt his manhood against me and it frightened me. I wasn't ready for sex and I definitely didn't want to have sex, wherever we were. He never pushed the issue; he just enjoyed having his way with me. And have his way with me he did; he pushed me beyond my limited sexual experience. Honestly why not have sex with him, since we had done so many other things? But we never did. These sessions were quick, one minute a passionate heat fest and the next he was gone. He would leave the room first, then I followed a few minutes later. I would always return to my room hot and bothered, wanting more of what I had left behind.

And so, our relationship lasted that semester, secret dates and make out sessions, which became more and more heated. No one ever knew we were a couple. We did a great job of hiding it. He never questioned me about anything and I didn't question him either. For me, I just didn't care who he was seeing or what he was doing. It didn't matter one bit to me. We never had an argument or a fight. Perfect right? Sure, if that's what you want but it wasn't what I wanted. I felt nothing for him. And I was sure he felt nothing for me. There were no feelings, no love, and honestly no relationship. I had accepted his rationale for keeping our involvement quiet. I can't even remember what his reason was now. But soon it all became clear to me that his reason was a lie. He didn't want anyone to know about me because I wasn't pretty enough. I wasn't the type of girl he could take home to his affluent parents. I simply wasn't good enough. It hurt so badly to know that someone had taken inventory of my appearance, my personality, and my heart and decided that I didn't measure up. It's not as if I didn't already feel this way before I met Spike, he was just the first person to confirm it.

The One

One evening at school I started to have chest pains while in the courtyard with some of my friends. They became quite frantic and called the ambulance. I can't recall much of what happened that night, but the one thing I will never forget was the paramedic. He was tall and light-skinned with deep, dark eyes. He had nice, full lips that were slightly covered by his mustache. He was absolutely gorgeous, and he was the first person I saw when I opened my eyes. And there I was staring up at him probably looking a mess. He told me everything was going to be fine and not to worry. I wasn't worried one bit. I must have been in and out of it a bit because I don't remember the ride to the hospital or much of what happened there. The gorgeous paramedic informed me of where I was and how I got there. He then asked me was I okay, but I couldn't find the words to speak. I nodded, "Yes," and he smiled down at me and then walked away. Now what I am about to tell you next is going to sound unbelievable, but it happened. My friends came in to check on me and I asked them who he was. As told to me by my friends, I went on and on about him. Everything turned out to be fine and I was soon released to go home. While in the car driving back to campus, my friends told me they had a surprise for me. I can't remember which friend it was that took my hand and slipped me a piece of paper. She said, "He said call him when you're feeling better." The gorgeous paramedic had given me his number.

I waited a couple of days before I called. I had no idea what I was going to say. I finally got up the nerve to call. The conversation was short but nice. We made plans to meet each other for a face-to-face. I asked him was it okay to bring a friend along and he agreed. A couple of days later my friend and I walked down the mountain to meet him at Hardees. I was so nervous. I had my friends pick out an outfit and shoes. We had agreed on a long, black shirt, green sweater, black boots, and a black hat. I was into hats back then. Anyway, my friend and I hiked down the mountain to Hardees. We made sure to leave early so we could be there before he was. He walked in a few minutes later and joined us at our table. The three of us talked for a while, then my friend stepped away to leave us alone. We chatted a bit and made plans to talk later. He told me I was pretty and he looked forward to getting to know me. These words sank in deep. There had never been a guy who had shown genuine interest in getting to know me. I didn't know how to let anyone get to know me on this level. Make out sessions I could do but just real conversation was quite new to me.

My paramedic loved to talk and I enjoyed listening to him. He called almost every day. He was a few years older than me, which didn't bother me at all. He had several jobs, an apartment and a car. He often came to campus and picked me up for dates. Sometimes we went out and other times we spent time at his apartment. We watched movies, other times we just sat and talked for hours. There were also times that my friend and her boyfriend double dated with us. No matter what we did, we always had a great time together. All of my friends knew about him, and his friends about me. It was the complete opposite of my so-called relationship with Spike. He was a true gentleman, the open your doors, pull out your chair kind of guy. There was never any pressure to push me out of my comfort zone. I had become quite guarded with my body after dealing with Spike. Sometimes I didn't even want to be touched, but he never complained. We spent a lot of time together and it wasn't long before I fell for him...and he for me.

    We soon made our relationship official. I finally had my first real legitimate relationship. I was over the moon happy and told anyone who would listen about my new boyfriend. I talked to my mother about him in letters and phone calls. Although I think she was somewhat skeptical because he was older, she was very happy for me. My friends were also very happy for me, but there was one person who wasn't too thrilled about my new relationship. Spike noticed that I wasn't always so readily available. Honestly, I don't know why I continued to deal with him at all after meeting my paramedic, but I did. I couldn't seem to bring myself to break free from him. I know it seems like a no-brainer, but it wasn't that easy for me. The only way I know how to explain is to say he seemed to have some sort of hold on me. I was afraid to make him mad. And he had a way of making me feel as though what I had with my paramedic wasn't real and wouldn't last. There was a huge part of me that believed him. My self-esteem wasn't any higher than it was in high school. And even though my paramedic had chosen me, there was still this sinking feeling that it was too good to be true. My dysfunctional relationship with Spike didn't help the situation either. Soon enough, I gathered the strength, better yet the courage, to end things with Spike. Strangely enough, he didn't want me nor did he want anyone else to have me.

My paramedic and I had a great relationship. I can't seem to remember us having an argument or fight about anything. Each time we spent together was better than the time before. With his job and my classes, there wasn't a lot of time for us to spend together. But every free moment we had, we spent together. I didn't realize it at the time but I was falling in love. It was an amazing feeling. He arrived before I did. I had some issues with trust, trusting him not to hurt me or me not to hurt myself by messing things up. I kept him at a distance as to be sure not to let him get too close too fast. I guarded my body like a fortress because I felt I had already given too much of myself away for someone else's pleasure. He didn't seem to mind that we weren't having sex; he just wanted me there with him and that was enough for me. As time passed we grew extremely close and very attached to one another. He wanted to touch me all the time, which I thoroughly enjoyed.

His touching wasn't necessarily sexual as much as it was intimate. There were many times I fell asleep in his arms, which was the best place on earth.

We had reached the point in our relationship where we started to plan our future. Although we had only been together a few months, we already knew that we wanted to spend the rest of our lives together. It was hard for me to accept that someone loved me so much that they wanted to spend their life with me. I was usually always the one falling hard and by myself. This time it was different; my love was reciprocated. Yes, everything was perfect until it wasn't.

It was during my second semester when I started to notice a change in my vision. There would be days of blurriness and then things would be clear again. It seemed to happen so slowly yet so fast and before I knew it, all the vision in my right eye was gone. Glaucoma can happen like that, so slow and steady that you don't even notice the change. But then so fast that there is nothing you can do to stop the loss. And the vision loss is irreversible! Needless to say, I freaked out. I was sure this was the end of college and my relationship. The thought of both was devastating. I soon had to leave Virginia and return to South Carolina for treatment. I had to take a medical withdrawal from school with hopes of returning the next semester. This meant leaving my paramedic behind. We spent as much time together as we could before I had to go.

My very last day was spent with my paramedic.

He came to pick me up early that morning. We went back to his apartment and talked about what was going to happen between us. We vowed to talk every day and visit one another as much as we could. He made plans to come to South Carolina as soon as possible. I promised to come back after Dr. Bobo fixed my eye. He kissed me deeply and passionately. Even now I can still remember knowing in that moment how much he truly loved me. That kiss took us to where I never planned to go. On that day, we made love. I was terrified but anxious. If I had to lose my virginity to anyone, he would definitely be that one. It felt so natural and I loved every moment of being with him. I completely trusted him with my heart. When it was all over, which didn't last as long as I thought it would, he held me close reminding me how much he loved me. I loved him so very much. For the first time, someone chose me, loved me, wanted me and I had to leave him. It didn't seem fair. He took me back to campus and we kissed goodbye. I cried, boy did I cry. I didn't want to leave him, but I held on to the hope that this wasn't the end for us. I couldn't imagine that life would be so different when I saw him again.

Chapter Six
Lesson Learned

I wasn't supposed to be there. I really wasn't supposed to be there. I knew that the moment I walked in. As I stood in the doorway of the small apartment I noticed all the guys there drinking, smoking and laughing. They seemed to be having a good time. They all said hello as I stood there not sure what to do next. Smoke filled my lungs. And the funky smell of cheap liquor filled the air. I gasped as I heard my grandmother's words echoing in my head. "Don't ever go over there PooPoo; nothing good goes on over there. Stay away from there." I should have left at that very moment, but I couldn't move because his eyes were fixed on me.

My body moved slowly, leaving common sense at the door as he reached for my hand. I went with him into the next room, a bedroom so we could talk without all the noise. I was flattered to be in his presence and felt comfortable enough because the place was filled with people. My mind ran wild with all the possibilities that this encounter could bring for us. I wasn't even sure of what I expected from him. I didn't want to be his girlfriend because he had far too many of those. Besides I wasn't the type of girl he dated. He was tall, dark and yes, very handsome. He was desired by most of the girls we went to school with. And as charming as he appeared to be, I'm fairly certain he had dated quite a few of them. So, what could possibly happen between us anyway? Plus, as much as I loved my mother, I didn't want history to repeat itself by getting pregnant by someone like him. So, sex was not an option. I didn't even want to have sex with him. So why was I there? O yea I know…because he noticed me and I needed to be noticed.

We talked for a little while, nothing too deep, just usual run of the mill talk. How are you? What's going on in your world? Who are you dating? Things like that. Of course, he said he wasn't dating anyone. I knew that to be a lie because he was always dating. I let him know that I was single but not interesting in dating because my heart was somewhere else. Not to mention I was still picking up the pieces after the bomb of blindness blew my life apart, but of course I didn't tell him that part. He told me I was pretty and he had always wanted to tell me that. Honestly as flattered as I should have been, I wasn't. It was mostly because I didn't believe him. I had reconciled with myself in the midst of his ramblings that I was satisfied that HE noticed me.

I think I got lost in my thoughts because I wasn't prepared for what happened next. He kissed me, hard and deep, so much so that I couldn't catch my breath. I tried to pull back a bit to get some air, but his grip was too tight. He had to feel me pulling but he didn't let go. I had been kissed before and I was sure that this kiss was different from any other. Was I flattered now? Yep, because HE was kissing me. But I also felt something else and I didn't like the other feeling. I felt afraid and all I heard was my grandmother's words screaming at me, "Don't ever go over there, PooPoo. Nothing good goes on over there. Stay away from there."

In a matter of seconds, I was pinned to the bed. He was heavy on top of me and the more I squirmed the harder he pressed. My eyes filled with tears but I couldn't make a sound. I was screaming but there was no sound. How could there be no sound? I knew the guys in the other room would come if I keep screaming but there was no sound. The music was too loud; they couldn't hear me. My mouth was opened wide but there was no sound. What was this hard lump under the pillow? Why was it making my head hurt? He kissed harder and deeper; I was choking but he wouldn't stop. Then he paused for a moment and looked at me. Then he began to tell me how he knew why I came and how I wanted what was about to happen next. He told me I should just give in because no one would ever believe that HE would have to take it from anyone. I told him I didn't want it and that's not why I came. Sobbing, I begged him to get off me and let me go. He didn't.

Time seemed to stand still as I laid there pinned down to the old, iron bed. So many thoughts were racing through my mind. I felt like my heart was going to burst from my chest. I couldn't breathe, but he didn't seem to care about my state of panic. I struggled to free myself from his grip. I squirmed and pushed underneath him, but he was much too heavy. The weight of his body on mine trapped me in a position I couldn't get out of. He started telling me how he knew I wanted this and I should just give in and enjoy it. He told me I was lucky to be there with him. I sobbed uncontrollable as I begged him not to hurt me. He told me this could be easy or hard, it was my choice. Before I knew it, he plunged hard and deep inside of me. It hurt. I tried to push upward away from him but he held me tighter. My head slipped between the iron bars of the bed pressed against the wall. The lump under the pillow was poking my neck and I was stuck. He continued to plunge deep and hard but slow as if we were making love. Then he began to push inward harder and faster. I screamed in pain, frustration and anger, but no one came.

Finally, after what seemed like forever, he released himself inside of me. The warmth of his fluids filled me and spilled out onto the bed. Tears flowed down my face and under my neck. My head hurt between the bars and the lump under the pillow seemed to be buried in my neck. He released his hold on me and allowed my head to be free from its unconformable position. He stayed on top of me, breathing deeply and heavy on my face. He stayed there, as I squirmed beneath him. He didn't move and I stopped squirming. There were no words, just heaving breathing and sobbing. He sat up and looked down at me. I just lay there unable to move. Every part of my body hurt. I knew I had to get out of there and back home before anyone knew I had left. I sat up slowly, never looking at him. I stood up to leave and started to walk slowly to the door. He called my name and I turned to look at him. He was sitting at the head of the bed. He reached under the pillow and pulled out a small black gun. He held it in his hand. That was the lump I felt under my head. He didn't say anything; he only held the gun and stared at me. I was so afraid, so very afraid. It was what he didn't say that scared me the most. It was as if he was issuing me a silent threat, but I heard it loud and clear. I walked out of the room and out of the apartment.

Once outside, I walked very slowly to my grandmother's apartment. The pain between my legs was preventing me from moving as fast as I wanted to. I wasn't too aware of who was outside. I prayed that my grandma and mom hadn't made it back home yet. There was no way that I could explain what just happened. No one was home. I went straight into the bathroom and took off all my clothes. I turned on the water for the shower as hot as I could stand it. I sat down in the shower and let the water run all over me. I cried and cried.

My grandmother kept a huge bar of brown soap that she used to take a bath. I remember her telling me that soap was also used for laundry back when she was young. I took that soap and scrubbed my skin all over. I washed so hard it hurt. I noticed that my white washcloth was turning a bright pink. There was dried blood between my legs. I scrubbed harder and harder trying to clean myself off. I got out of the shower, put on lotion and dressed in some sweats and a t-shirt. I went to the bathroom and gathered up my clothes. That's when I noticed the blood all over my underwear. I was horrified. I put the clothes in a plastic bag, tied it up and took them outside to the dumpster. I went back inside and laid on the couch. My mind raced with everything that had happened. I felt guilty, stupid and extremely dirty, even though I scrubbed my skin off.

Soon my mother and grandma were back from the store. They didn't even notice I had changed clothes. I listened as they chatted together in the kitchen, but all I could seem to hear was "Don't ever go over there, PooPoo. Nothing good goes on over there." Grandma was right; nothing good happened there. I was never going back and no one will ever know I went.

I don't remember much about the days that followed. There are only a few things that come to mind as I am writing. One of which are the many showers I took. I felt so extremely dirty and I just wanted to wash it all away. But it seemed the more showers I took, the worse I felt. I couldn't wash away the memories that played over and over in my mind. I was afraid all the time. I didn't want to go outside because I knew he was somewhere out there. I never wanted to see him again. I didn't want him to see me either. I wondered what he thought of me. I wondered if he knew what he took from me. Did he even care? He didn't seem like the type that would care. He probably felt like he did me a favor or I was lucky that HE would even be with me. He was wrong. I didn't feel lucky. I felt incredibly stupid. I knew better than to be there. How could I let this happen? It was all my fault.

My mother had taught me how to handle such situations. She warned me about boys and what they expected from a girl. She warned me this could happen if I put myself in this situation. Why didn't I listen? These thoughts raced through my head everyday along with what seemed like a million more of would've, could've, should've. No one noticed the change in me. And that was how I wanted it. I didn't want to have to answer anyone's questions. So, I pretended to be okay and tried to act as normal as I could to avoid suspicion. But the pressure was about to break me in two. I needed to tell someone. I had to get this off my chest.

What I wanted to do was run to my father, and no I don't mean Teddy. I wanted to tell the man who gave me life, the one that was supposed to protect me and keep me safe. In my mind, I would tell him and he would be so angry that someone had hurt me that way. He would hold me close as I released all the hurt and pain through my tears. He would tell me everything would be okay as he plotted how he would kill the offender in his head. Maybe he would shoot him over and over until there were no more bullets in his gun. Or maybe he would stab him until his arm got tired. Or maybe he would just torture him until he begged for death. Yep, my father would make him pay dearly for hurting his little girl. My father would kill him, he would be dead, and I would be happy again, only if there was a father who cared enough. There wasn't and that thought alone only drove the pain and despair in deeper.

So, I went to the one person I trusted most. Talking on the phone was for the best. I didn't want to have to face him while I told him what happened. I didn't want to see that look of helplessness or anger on his face. I really didn't know what to expect; I only knew I didn't want to see it. It took me awhile to get up the nerve to make the call but I eventually did. I went into my grandma's room and lay across the bed to make the call. When he answered, he could tell something was wrong. He just knew me that well. I didn't bother lying or pretending with him. I just started talking and the story poured out of me like word vomit. I didn't stop talking until the ache in my stomach was gone. I finished and there was silence. Actually, there was silence for quite some time. Finally, the silence was broken by a very unfamiliar tone. He sounded cold as he began to explain to me why what happened to be was indeed my fault. No, he didn't say those words exactly, but he implied it. I'm pretty sure it wasn't his intention to make me feel worse, but he did. He was right, what did I think was going to happen when I followed him into that room? I couldn't take the chance of trying to explain this to anyone else, so I decided to keep quiet and bury it.

That was easier said than done. I had nightmares almost every night. I didn't want to go outside because I didn't want to run into him anywhere. I couldn't pray because I was so angry at myself for being so stupid. So, I was sure God was mad at me, too. I didn't know how to move pass the pain and betrayal I felt. It hurt to even think about that day. It hurt to look in the mirror. There was a constant ache in my soul that I couldn't put into words. I hated myself more than I had before. How could anyone ever love me now? On top of all the other baggage I carried, this only made it harder for someone to accept me. I didn't love me so how could anyone else? I needed a way out of the pain and the memories. I couldn't breathe inside the self-created bubble I put myself in. So many other horrible thoughts occupied my mind. One thought in particular loomed in the back of my mind. What if I were pregnant? It had been almost two weeks and I hadn't had a menstrual cycle. I didn't keep track of it like I should since I only had sex the one time. But paranoia started to set in. There was no way I was going to have HIS baby and be tied to him forever. I already knew that I would have an abortion if I were pregnant, but I couldn't stay at home. It was time for a change of scenery and I knew just where I wanted to go.

New York

In case you hadn't noticed, I never made it back to Virginia. My vision loss was irreversible and I had no idea of what to do with myself. I never told my paramedic what happened to me. We slowly drifted apart because I shut down completely. I couldn't feel anything, not even his unconditional love for me or mine for him. All I knew is that I had to go.

    My aunt and uncle who brought my cousins down south most summers lived in Buffalo, New York. My cousins and I were very close and I looked forward to seeing them every year. I had always wanted to go to New York to visit them, but it never seemed to be the right time. Well, now was the perfect time to make the trip and so I informed my mother I would be leaving for a while. My mother was very nervous about me flying to New York alone. This was the first time I had ever flown, not to mention the circumstances had changed tremendously from the times I had asked to go before. This time I didn't need her permission because I was an adult. However, I was now a legally blind adult, which would make the trip a bit more difficult. I wasn't afraid at all. Okay, maybe just a little.

    I had no problem making the airline aware of my disability. They were quite accommodating. There I was sitting in the terminal waiting to board the plane. I was excited about the trip. I looked forward to seeing my family and the good times I knew we would have together. More than anything, I was relieved to be leaving the place that reminded me of that awful day. I thought putting some distance between me and that place would help. The truth is, although it was a little easier, the pain remained. No matter where I was going, my memories went with me. There was no escaping those. I hugged and kissed my mother goodbye and boarded the plane. Who knew that this adventure would change my life forever!

Buffalo NY was no McCormick by a longshot, not that I expected it to be. I had heard the stories from my cousins of how rough and dangerous it could be. I just didn't expect it to look rough. The houses were all in a nice, neat row, separated into blocks. There wasn't a lot of grass, just sidewalks and concrete. The air even seemed different, not as clean as back home. There were a lot of people walking this way and that way. I spoke to everyone I saw, which I later learned was not a good idea. People in New York weren't as friendly as they were down South. Everyone had their group that they were apart of and they pretty much stuck to them. I couldn't wear certain colors on certain blocks because colors represented groups or territories. It was all quite confusing to me but very interesting.

I loved the convenience of everything. There was a store on almost every corner. We could take the city bus or train and be wherever we needed to be in a matter of minutes. My cousins and I had a great time together. They enjoyed showing me their city and I had fun seeing it. My aunt and uncle made me feel welcomed. It was almost like I was a part of a new family. I had almost forgotten the reason I ran away. But late at night when I tried to sleep, the nightmares reminded me of a reality I couldn't escape.

I stayed in NY for about a month or so. During this time, I hung out with my older cousin and met some of her friends. I met a couple of different guys that we hung out with from time to time, but nothing became serious. I wasn't focused on dating at this point. I was afraid to trust a guy with any part of me, so I remained distant and unobtainable. Besides, most of my heart was still in Lynchburg, Virginia and the piece that I kept to myself was dark because of what had happened to me. I'm pretty certain that it has been noted that I can't bring myself to say the word. Even after all this time, it's still hard to say.

As time passed and my menstrual cycle showed up the fear began to disappear. Now that there was no baby to worry about, maybe I could put the whole thing behind me. There was no tangible proof that the incident ever occurred and for that I was very grateful. I wasn't prepared to have an abortion or to explain why I needed one. So, I tried very hard to forget, the nightmares even decreased but something had changed in me forever. I just didn't know how much.

While meeting someone was the farthest thing from my mind, that is exactly what happened during the Spring of 1994 right before I was scheduled to go back to South Carolina. One day, my younger cousin and I were prank calling random numbers. Juvenile, yes, I know, but we were bored. Back then, most people (guys especially) had pagers. So, we would just make up a number and call. Sometimes guys called back and sometimes not. But there was this one guy who did call back. This time when the phone rang, my cousin passed it to me. I was a little nervous because I had no idea what to say to him. But he wasn't the least bit shy and kept the conversation going. He asked me if it was okay for him to keep in touch. I was like sure, why not, what did I have to lose. He seemed nice enough, so we made plans to talk later. Honestly, past experiences had taught me not to get my hopes up about guys and so I didn't expect to hear from him again. But he fooled me.

He called me every day. And we talked for hours about everything and nothing. I enjoyed talking to him because he was different from any other guy I had talked to in the past, not that there were many. He was a straight shooter. He always said exactly what was on his mind with no regard for how it came out or who it would affect. He was overly confident, thought he was the best-looking guy in the entire world. There was no convincing him otherwise. And although it got on my nerves at time, I admired his high self-esteem. I often told him he was conceded, but he called it convinced.

After some time, we finally met in person. My aunt was not happy about the young thug that I had invited into her home. But I didn't care because I was falling for him hard. He was medium height, dark brown-skinned, and had beautiful brown eyes. He was kind of stocky and solid. He was dressed in baggy purple shorts, an oversized Tupac t-shirt, black and white Nikes and a fitted cap. He looked just as confident as he said he was. He invited himself in and we took a seat in the living room. There we sat with his arm around me like he was letting my family know that I belonged to him. It was nice, the warm feeling that was creeping up my spine. And although he was nothing like anyone would have chosen for me, I liked him if for that reason alone.

Our first meeting was nice and we had a good time. We hung out a few more times after that, but soon I had to go back home. It was a bittersweet feeling. I was ready to go home because I missed the simple country life, but I wasn't ready to leave the excitement of NY or the thug that came along with it. We had already talked about me making another trip back to NY. My mother had no idea why I was so anxious to return, but my aunt did and she wasn't happy about it. She made it very clear that she didn't like "City Slicker," which was her name for him. She didn't want us seeing each other. I made it clear that I didn't care what she thought and I was going to continue seeing him.

Soon I returned to McCormick and everyone assumed that would be the end of our little romance, but boy were they wrong. We wrote letters, sent cards, and talked on the phone for hours almost every night. We made plans for my return trip to NY and his first trip to SC. It was all so exciting…we were falling in love.

I couldn't wait to return to Buffalo to see my thug. I was barely at home a whole month before I left again. My mother was curious about the guy who was sending me letters, cards and calling almost every night. She soon concluded that this mystery guy was the reason I was in such a hurry to get back to New York, and of course she was right. But I didn't let her know that.

When I arrived back in Buffalo, he couldn't wait to see me. I tried to play down my excitement to my family, but I couldn't wait to see him either. We got the opportunity to spend a lot of time together while I was there. He would come over sometimes, which my aunt hated. And other times, we went out. And almost every time I was with him in public, there was some girl giving me the ugly face. You know the face when the lips are all twisted, nose "turnt" up, and piercing eyes staring as if to say "I hate you," without even knowing who you are. But he would always say, "Don't worry about her, she aint nobody." So, I didn't. Besides he was known as the "The Ladies' Man," whether it was self-proclaimed or otherwise. Either way, with his popularity I should have expected some jealousy. But who cared? He was mine...all mine.

Then, the day I was trying desperately to avoid finally came. I had managed to keep things G-rated for the most part because I was nowhere near ready for anything more. However, this day things went further than I had planned, way faster than I had planned. And although I don't remember the event in its entirety, I do remember the post emotional breakdown that took place in my head. I screamed inside, much like I had done on that dreadful day. But this time, I didn't open my mouth and he had no clue of what was going on inside of me. How did I get here? Is this really about to happen again? What if I say no? Will he stop? Will he hurt me? How do I get out of here? I was gripped with fear, so, so, so very afraid. I couldn't see any way out. I didn't know what to do to save myself. My soul cried as I tried desperately to get my thoughts together. And against all the thoughts in my head, all the fear in my heart, and everything that was telling me NO…I surrendered. I gave myself to him that day, not because I loved him so much or because I wanted to but because I refused to let anyone else take something from me. So, New York and I had sex that day, which was extremely different from making love and I didn't like it at all.

Thinking back on it now, I realized that things moved rather quickly. And yet I did nothing to stop them. I had left one amazing boyfriend that I loved dearly and met another that I was falling hard for. I was conflicted because I felt an obligation to keep the promises I made to my paramedic, but then I was afraid that he couldn't handle what I was facing. Losing my vision took a toll on me and there was no one I had to share that with. Although I still had vision in my left eye, it wasn't as strong as it had been before. My newly built confidence had already been shattered, but now it was destroyed. And instead of working to build it on my own, I once again had turned to the attention and approval of yet another guy. Never mind the fact that I had a faithful guy still waiting for me to return to Virginia: I had a new one wanting to build a life with me. Truth is I should have gone back to Virginia to what God had given me despite all that had happened. That's where my heart was. But I no longer felt like the girl who had fallen in love with the handsome paramedic. I was different. New York didn't know the girl before the blindness, before the dreadful day that killed her. He had fallen for the pieces that remained and those pieces latched on to him. I let myself down and therefore, I was responsible for the murder of my soul. Yes, I know I am not supposed to blame myself, but I did. My disobedience cost me everything.

Chapter Seven
Growing Pains

In the blink of an eye, he had moved to South Carolina to live. He moved his whole life to be with me. If that wasn't love, I didn't know what was. There's no way you could have convinced me that he wasn't my second chance. And believe me, I had people lined up trying to convince me and leading the line was my mother. See, it was fine when he and I were just writing letters and talking on the phone. But it was a very different thing when he was in my mother's space and "taking her baby girl," as she would put it. It was no secret that my mother did not like him; well that's probably because she made it known. She was also quite angry with my grandmother and auntie for bringing him here. I didn't care how she felt and I let her know that she had a choice, accept him or I would move to NY. Needless to say, she wasn't very happy with that at all. There were times I could be just as stubborn as my mother, and this was one of those times. I was willing to give up EVERYTHING for him. My mother figured that out quickly and decided that she couldn't run the risk of losing her only child, so if that meant accepting him that's what she would do. Although her acceptance of him was a slow process that would soon have to speed up real fast.

He was a different kind of guy. He dressed

differently, talked differently, walked differently, and acted quite differently from any other guy I had met. He had a different type of attitude and way of thinking. He was street-minded and wise with the kind of wisdom that only comes from life experience. He had seen things and done things that I only saw on television. He knew things and had a very different view of the world. He was good and kind. He was brutally honest and straight forward. He didn't bite his tongue for anyone, not even my mother. He always said exactly what he wanted, whenever he wanted, and to whomever he wanted. But there was a side of him that he rarely showed the world that I thought was on reserve just for me. It was his tender side. He was compassionate and empathetic towards me. He never saw my visual impairment as a disability. He was able to look past it to my heart. I didn't think that was possible.

    Everyone in McCormick took notice of the mysterious new guy. Walking through town in his baggy attire with a lock and chain around his neck, he couldn't help but draw attention to himself. He wasn't fazed by the attention at all. I think he liked it. He was the polar opposite of me, a breath of fresh air. But it was the rule of opposites attracts that pulled me to him like a magnet. I loved him so deeply, completely and uncontrollably. There were times when I felt that I loved him too much, but I didn't know how to contain it. I wanted to be with him all the time, which I knew had to be smothering. He never said a word. I needed to feel close to him. He made me feel safe and protected like nothing or no one could ever hurt me. I desperately needed that. He also made me so very happy and with him I was able to forget. I could forget what I lost and what I had given away. He was my chance at a new start. He had no idea of the weight that came with loving me.... neither did I.

For a while New York and I bounced back and forth between my aunt's house and my grandmother's house. We tried not to stay with grandma too often because she had the tendency to kick us out at a moment's notice if she was having her gentlemen friend come over, which was way more often than I care to think about. By this time my mother had finally left Teddy and in doing so, she sold my childhood home. She was now working two full-time jobs in nearby Greenwood SC, at the hospital during the day and patient-sitting at night. She only came down on the weekends. So basically, New York and I were homeless.

Neither of us liked the feeling of being at another person's mercy, nor did it leave us much time to be alone. In fact, we were rarely ever alone. But we found creative ways to be together. And when we were together it was amazing. Maybe it was the thrill of almost getting caught that made the sex so great. Or maybe it was because I had convinced myself it had to be great verses the alternative. The truth is sex became a habit, something I felt like I was supposed do, better yet needed to do... just like I did the very first time.

The very first time New York and I had sex took me back to a place I never wanted to go again, a place I now only visited in my nightmares. Actually, it felt as if I was right back in that tiny apartment full of noisy people that couldn't hear me. This time the apartment was in Buffalo, New York filled with people who didn't even know who I was. This time I was nowhere near the safety of my grandmother's home. This time there would be nowhere for me to run. I remember staring in his face praying that he wouldn't hurt me or at least notice the look of terror that had to be shining brightly there. I didn't want was about to happen. He had no clue and I couldn't let him know. Fear paralyzed me. He probably thought I was nervous, he had no idea what was going on in my head. Something clicked in me. I wasn't going to let anyone else take anything else from me. So, this time I made the decision to surrender willingly. I let it happen although it was the last thing I wanted. It was too soon. I wasn't ready. I didn't want to be touched. So why didn't I just tell him that? Well, I honestly have no idea. I didn't feel anything, no emotion at all. I was expecting the familiar feeling of love and acceptance like that of which I shared with my paramedic, (who still lingered in my heart and mind) but it never came. It was probably because I wasn't in love with this guy and I didn't feel like he loved me either. We barely knew each other well enough for what was about to happen. But I told myself this is what I had to do and that all the feelings and emotions would come soon enough, so

I sacrificed myself again. I told myself if I do this he will love me, he will accept me, and maybe just maybe I won't feel so dirty.

I let myself float away from that moment, therefore I can't remember the details of my first time with New York. Although it seemed like forever, I recall it being over rather quickly and I was glad for that. I kept my secret for a while longer while allowing sex to become a normal part of my developing relationship with him. However, nothing was normal about it to me, but I learned to pretend to enjoy it. I made it a point to try and get good at it and even initiate it at times. Eventually I was hooked and started to enjoy it…maybe a little bit too much.

It wasn't long before New York and I got a place of our own. It was a small one-bedroom apartment up the hill from my grandmother. It turns out that being legally blind had its perks. I received SSI (Supplementary Security Income) for my disability. I was also able to get the apartment at a discounted rate based on my income (which wasn't very much). New York had also found a job by now, so we were okay. While my mother hated the idea of me "shacking up" with a man that wasn't my husband, she helped us get furniture and other things we needed for the apartment. Truth is, living with a man that wasn't my husband went against everything I believed in. I didn't want things to start this way, but the thought of having the love I so desperately wanted was all worth it, even if it was "out of order." Love had clouded my judgement to the point where I was willing to throw my morals away if it got my desired results. Things were starting to get serious with New York by this time. Time seemed to fly by and everything was moving at an accelerated speed. I went there, he moved here, and then we lived together all in a matter of months. It's safe to assume that neither of us gave much thought of the future; we truly did live in the moment.

Our love was intoxicating to me. It was an all-consuming feeling. I'm not sure if he was feeling what I was feeling. All I knew was that he was it for me, the one I wanted to spend all my time with...the rest of my life with. I poured myself into him. I was totally devoted to him. When he came home from work, I ran out to greet him, wrapping my arms around his neck. All his coworkers watched from the van that dropped him off, but I didn't care one bit. I'm not sure if he did and I didn't care. I cooked, cleaned and took care of him the best way I knew how to at nineteen. We spent hours talking and getting to know each other deeper and deeper. He was easy to talk to and I found myself trusting him with parts of me that I thought impossible to share. I can honestly say he became my very best friend. He was my everything, the focus of my life. I felt as if I didn't have anything else. I gave myself willingly to him now, mind, soul, and especially body, as much as he wanted and as often as he wanted. It was insane the way we made love and it was a high in which I can't explain. I was addicted to the feeling that sex gave me, I felt powerful, desired but mostly I felt in control. And I loved being in control. I was lost in him, or the idea of what I needed him to be for me. Did he love me? I'm sure he did based on whatever he knew love to be. And I loved him in a way that I thought love should be, but I'm not sure it was healthy for either of us.

I can honestly say I tested his love far beyond what seems reasonable to me now. I didn't mean to but then again there were times I think I knew exactly what I was doing. I would have these "fits" where I would lash out at him because I was afraid he was going to hurt me. These moments were real to me. My mind took me to a place where I felt threatened. I guess the best way to explain it is to say my nightmares were happening when I was awake. I would be right back in that apartment, right back in that room and I felt I had to fight my way out. I can even remember having a knife once telling him to stay away. By this time, he knew all about what happened to me earlier that year. So, he just calmly reminded me I was safe and that he would never hurt me. Other times when I had issues with my health, I may have exaggerated the problem to see if he cared. His worry would always assure me that he did. There was one particular time I was having chest pains, nothing serious; it could have been indigestion for all I knew, but he thought it was my heart. So, I went with it. He was so scared I was going to die that he cried and begged me not to leave him. The tears in his eyes made my heart melt and I knew his love was real. Why didn't I know before then? I don't know. He showed me the only way he could.

After a trip to the hospital, a long wait in the emergency room, and a battery of unnecessary tests, I was sent home with a clean bill of health. I knew I was fine but never said a word. Many tests would come after this, some intentional and others unintentional by no control of my own. He still stayed. I didn't deserve him and I knew it, but I tried to be better as we grew deeper in love. And we did grow deeper in love to the point where there was no test needed.

To say that we were naïve and irresponsible is an understatement. While we were busy falling in love and having free-will sex every day, we never considered all the risks we were taking. We were aware of the others sexual history and felt comfortable not using any form of protection. Yet and still I had no clue of what diseases may have been running wild in his body nor he in mine. We didn't think to get tested or to take precautions against all the things that could occur from unprotected sex. Needless to say, I wasn't on any form of birth control either, just plain careless! As a matter of fact, other than the "don't have sex until you're married" conversation, my mother and I didn't talk about sex. Of course, I knew all about birth control, condoms, and how important it was to protect yourself from a sex education class at school. It was very easy to walk into any county health department to ask to be put on birth control or get free condoms. For some stupid irresponsible reason, I chose not to do so. And as you may well guess by now, I have no good excuse for that either. I guess I was like millions of other teenagers thinking nothing bad was going to happen to me; boy was I wrong about that one. We ended up having Chlamydia, which is and STD treated by an oral medication. As mad as I wanted to be mad, I couldn't be because we weren't sure who gave it to whom. Not to mention it was my responsibility to protect myself and I didn't. We just got it treated and kept it moving.

You would think that our little STD situation would prompt us to be more careful, use a little more wisdom or show a bit more responsibility. It did not. We just kept moving carelessly along through our teenage lives. Although personally I was sort of worried that something else could be lingering out there, I didn't mention it to New York. Besides, the original examinations tested for all STDs and nothing else popped up, so I assumed we were good. And we were. I was happy with life as it had become. I found things to do all day while New York was working. Yet I did miss school and the friends I had made there. I also missed the friends I had at home who were off living their college lives. But I had something that they didn't at that time, I had love. Strange thing is, this love thing never made me think of the future. I didn't give much consideration to what I was going to do with my life. Before there was a New York or even a Paramedic, I had big plans for my future. I was going to be a Psychologist.... Dr. Liquinita Callaham! But losing my vision changed all of that and left me with yet another void that I didn't know how to fill. I knew that I wanted more than love. I wanted to be someone and do something. Well, soon enough I was going to be someone and have a whole lot to do because as of November 1994 we were going to have a baby!!!!

New York was over the moon with happiness. Apparently having a child, a daughter to be precise, was a secret desire of his. As a matter of fact, impregnating me was all a part of a plan he had going on in his head. You can be sure that I wasn't made aware of this plan and I wasn't as over the moon as he was. Honestly, I was nowhere near the moon. I was mad as hell, at him, at me and at my cousin who had talked me into taking the dumb test in the first place. She was the one who wanted the kid, not me, but that's another story for another time. Anyway, let's get back to me; I didn't want to be anyone's mother. I didn't want to hand over my life to anyone else. I had just given myself to him and now he was expecting me to give myself to someone else. I would like to think I could be as selfless as my mother had always been, but I think I was more selfish than selfless. Not to mention I was scared, not of being a mother but of telling my mother that I was pregnant. I knew that was a conversation that I didn't want to have. I was sure that her strong dislike for New York would skyrocket into full blown hatred. Nope I wasn't going to tell her and you know what, I never did!

My mother didn't react exactly as I thought she would. She wasn't at all happy when my grandmother gave her the news, but she accepted it.

She wasn't angry but she was quite disappointed. She was disappointed because I knew to make better choices for myself. She was also disappointed because the father of my child wasn't my husband and she wasn't alone in that. Although I never saw myself as a mother, I never saw myself as being one without a husband. I would like to say it was because it wasn't the Godly order of things, but that wasn't the primary reason. If I were to be a mother it was going to be with a husband, one who was biologically connected to my child. I just wanted something different than what I grew up with, and if I couldn't have different then I didn't want it at all. I didn't know what kind of father New York would be. I didn't know if he could give our daughter (yep he got his girl...spoiler) all the things daddies are supposed to give daughters. But I guess we were going to find out soon enough.

At this point in my life, I found my mind drifting, as it often did in certain situations, back to my father. I wonder how he would feel knowing that his baby girl was going to become a mother? Would he be angry? Happy? Disappointed? Word on the street is that he was already a grandfather, so I guess it wouldn't have made much difference to him. But I still couldn't help but wonder what he would think of me having a child. He wasn't my only concern; I was going to have to have a conversation with my pastor, which scared me more than telling my mother. Pastor was the closest man I had to a father. He was good at it, too! Although he had a family of his own, he still made room in his heart for all of his "church children." His opinion meant a lot to me and I knew he would be hurt and very disappointed. And he was, but he was also surprisingly supportive as I imagined a father should be. He reminded me that he still loved me, God still loved me and He still had a purpose for my life. I needed to hear that because I did feel bad for letting God down. I had given my life to Him some time ago and I know I was required to live my life according to His Word, but I wasn't always good at that. See my relationship with God was kind of complicated. I believed in Him and tried my best to live in a way I thought pleasing to Him. However, I didn't view Him as the father many Christians referred to Him as. I tried but I just couldn't ever seem to get that part down. Certainly it had a lot to do with the desire I carried for my earthly father. So, I guess with that being said, I had trouble with the whole obedience part of the father/daughter relationship when it came to God. In any case, it was good to know that I hadn't completely let God down with all my sinful behavior.

There were concerns that pregnancy would put extra pressure on my heart. Some even thought that having a baby would kill me and wondered why I put myself in such a position. It's funny because of all the things racing through my mind, that thought wasn't even in the number. The doctors never told me I couldn't have children or that if I did it would cause problems. I also can't ever recall asking the question either, mainly because I never thought of having children. The question has often been asked whether I considered an abortion at the time. The truth is, the thought never crossed my mind. Of all things, I knew I was already doing wrong. I didn't want to add child murder to the list. Yes, I know it's a mother's right to choose, but abortion was never a choice for me....it just wasn't. I had other concerns, such as how much was this going to hurt? Or how was I going to provide for this kid? Would I be a good mother? Did I know how? Of course, I knew how because I had the greatest mother in the universe. But did I have what she had? Could I do it as well and easily as she had? Those were the questions I lay in bed thinking about. All in knew for sure is that she was on her way and we had to get ready!

The months seemed to zoom by. I was getting bigger and bigger by the day. I was always sleepy and hungry. I can't remember feeling much else. I was mean to everyone. I don't know why but everything and everyone aggravated me. But everyone was quite understanding, especially New York, who most definitely caught the worst of my wrath. He handled me well though. He made sure I had everything I needed and most of what I wanted. He tolerated my sleepless nights and annoying cravings (mostly Big Macs). He was so excited, which soon rubbed off on me. My mother threw me a beautiful, baby shower, which profited me much. All my closest friends and family were there. Teddy even showed up. By this time our relationship was quite the complicated one, but he was trying. I received so many much-needed gifts. I received a huge package from my college roommate that took it over the top. We didn't have to buy much at all. New York and I were happy. Mommy was happy, which made things a lot easier. Everything was falling into place. Everything was all set for her arrival. And on August 1, 1995, we welcomed Alexis Xzarria into our world!!!

Alexis, the name her daddy chose for her, Xzarria the name I chose for her, and her last name was that of her father. She was the most beautiful little person I have ever seen in my life. This was love, the real true kind! The kind of love that made your heart burst with joy. This must have been what my mother tried to explain to me, she's right; there are no words to express what I was feeling. I loved her so much. I knew from the moment they placed her in my arms that I would give my life for her. I couldn't imagine my life without this little person I just met. In that instant, she became my entire world, sole purpose for being, and all that I could have ever hoped for. I couldn't stop staring at her.... she was love!

I enjoyed my first couple of days in the hospital with my baby. I had to stay longer because I had a Caesarean-Section, and the doctors needed to keep an eye on me. Alexis stayed with me most of the day and slept in the nursery at night. She was a perfect little being, soft and she smelled so good. She had silky black hair, the cutest little button nose, and the prettiest, dark eyes. Her eyes danced around whenever she was awake, as if she was checking out her surroundings. Her tiny hand was always wrapped around my finger when I held her. She was a perfect angel and I was in love! New York was there when he got off from work. He was a proud father. His face lit up every time he saw her. Watching him interact with her put my heart at ease. I knew he would be a great father, he fell in love with her, just as I did. Now it was the three of us, our own little family. I was so excited to take her home and start our lives together. I could tell New York was excited too, although he didn't express it as much. Sometime he could be that strong silent type, and you never knew what he was thinking. But I knew he was happy and that made me happy. Nope, this wasn't a part of the plan, at least not mine but I think it was the best blessing we could have asked for.

It was the day that we were to be discharged, I was packed and ready to go, just waiting to sign my release papers. The nurse came in to make sure I had everything and gave me final instructions for my care after I was released. But then she said something that threw me for a loop, "There are courtesy rooms available if you want to stay and be close to your baby," she said.

"Why would I need a courtesy room; we are being discharged today?" I asked. She stared blankly at me then excused herself from the room. I looked at New York with panic and confusion; he just stood there staring just as blankly as the nurse had. My mind was racing frantically. What's wrong? What's wrong? God please let her be okay. Soon after the nurse returned with a doctor. Before he even spoke a word, there was a sinking knot in my stomach that hurt so badly and then tears started flowing uncontrollably. We weren't prepared for what we were about to hear. "I'm sorry but your daughter has holes in her heart, and she will have to have open-heart surgery," the doctor said.

My heart sank and the tears continued to flow. New York stood still, stoned-faced as if he refused to show any emotion. He placed himself next to me and tried to comfort me. But it was the words that followed that landed the devastating blow that would change our lives forever. "Your daughter is also blind," he said. New York broke and my heart shattered.

Chapter Eight
Test of Faith

The days and months to follow are all a blur to me as I look back on that time in my life. Things took off so fast that I can barely remember in what order everything occurred. We left Self Memorial Hospital that day and headed for the Medical College of Georgia, the same place my mother had found herself with me twenty years earlier. And she was right there with me as I walked out the steps of her life. I think she was the most impacted by what was happening with Alexis. Here, she was reliving the exact same nightmare all over again with her granddaughter as she had with her daughter. I knew she was hurting, but she hid it well to be strong for me. I desperately needed her strength. I was a total wreck! I was still in pain from the C-Section, but I didn't have time to go home and rest. I didn't want to go home without my baby. I had to be with my baby, wherever she was, there I would be also. I had no intention of leaving her side, and I didn't. It was especially hard for New York because he wanted to be there with us, but he had to work. We couldn't afford for him to lose his job. He was there as much as he could be, and I tried to reassure him that I was holding things together. Truth is, I selfishly didn't care about his job or that we needed the money, I wanted him there with me.

He was stronger than I was, and if by chance he wasn't, he did a good job of hiding it from me. I can't recall ever seeing him pray, but I was sure that he was praying. I don't remember ever seeing him cry again after that first day, but I knew he was hurting. I know his heart was broken but he was always faithful and hopeful that things were going to be just fine. As for me, I struggled. God and I had many conversations about Alexis; it was more so me pleading for Him to spare her life. I can't ever remember Him talking back to me. (And yes, I do believe God talks to me.) I spent many days praying and crying. I won't lie and say I never question God because I did many times. As a matter of fact, I was angry, angry that He had allowed this to happen to my baby. I didn't understand why and I felt like I was being punished for all my wrong doings. There were times that I didn't say anything to God at all, I just cried.

Alexis' issues with her heart were different from mine. Actually, the doctors say they were less complicated. Technology had come a long way in twenty years and so the holes in her heart could be easily repaired. However, the problem came in with her being so small and not eating a lot. The actual process of eating took too much work for her. She would suck and stop, suck and stop all the while breathing heavily. I watched her struggling and I felt completely helpless. She would tire out easily, therefore she wouldn't eat. She wasn't gaining weight fast enough and they couldn't do the surgery until she was bigger and stronger. And if they couldn't fix her heart yet, then the eyes would have to wait. We were at a standstill for quite a while.

After some time, she was given a feeding tube so she wouldn't have to work so hard to eat. That was a struggle within itself because she was constantly yanking the tube out. The doctors finally decided to tie her tiny hands down, which was terrible for me to watch. She cried a lot which made her very tired, which made her little heart work overtime. As soon as she started to gain some weight, she caught an infection, which prolonged things even more. My heart broke a little more each day as I watched her fight for every breath she took. This must have been what my mother felt watching me. I knew that if I lost my baby, I would die. I didn't want to live without her...she was my life.

Time passed and the infection cleared and she got stronger. She had her first open heart surgery when she was three-months-old. There were prayers and well-wishes pouring in from family, friends, and church members. We prayed for the best. There were so many thoughts racing through my head. At the back were thoughts of my father who seemed to always be there when I was going through certain times in my life. You know those times when a daughter could use her father, if only just to hold her and tell her everything was going to be okay. He probably didn't even know I had given birth. Why should I care if he didn't? But I did. I wanted him here with me too, but I knew that was not even a possibility. How could he be there for a granddaughter he didn't even know he had if he couldn't be bothered to be there for a daughter he knew he had? It wasn't easy but I had to put him out of my mind. My thoughts needed to be focused on my baby.

Alexis was still rather small, so it was a delicate process. There were some touch and go moments; we came so close to losing her. I can recall this one time my family talked me into going home. New York and I were exhausted from all the back and forth. I just wanted to sleep, but then the phone rang. They called and told us she was in distress and they were going to have to go back in. They didn't know if she was going to make it. We raced from McCormick to Augusta; I prayed the entire way there. I begged God to please not take my baby! Please God don't let her die! And He didn't, she pulled through. Her recovery was slow but steady. They told us she would have to have another surgery when she was older. I was just thankful to God that she survived this one.

After about a couple of weeks or so we were allowed to take Alexis home. We had to get her ready for the eye surgery that she would be having soon. We were referred to a doctor in Charleston, SC for the best care for her eyes. Her eye condition was significantly worse than mine. There had been some serious issues with the optic nerve and she was born with Glaucoma and cataracts. One of her eyes never completed the developmental process, so there was only one eye left to work with. They were going to remove the cataracts and give her implants to control the pressure and strengthen her vision. She would have to have several more operations to repair the damage to the remaining eye. They had gone unattended so long that some of the damage was irrevocable.

You would think that I would be more concerned with her heart issues than those with her eyes, but it was quite the opposite. I knew that the repairs to the heart would be successful and hidden, but the eye issues were external. That stirred up a heap of emotions for me. I can't say what was going on in New York's head. I wondered if he blamed me for what was happening to our daughter? I wondered if he regretted getting into this relationship with me? I wondered if he would abandon us like my father abandoned my mother and me? God, why did every issue in my life lead back to my missing father? I truly hated him for that. However, my deepest fears were of how the world would treat my precious baby. All I could think about was how cruelly I was treated, all the name calling, relentless teasing, and how much it hurt. I didn't want that kind of pain for her. I wanted to shield her from that, but there was no way I could. And what was worse for me is that her eye issues were noticeable. Her left eye was discolored with a cloudy like tint to it. She had no vision at all in it. I felt that would make her a target far more than my coke bottle glasses made me. Every time I thought back to what I endured as a child, my heart broke all over again.

New York was great through all of this. He was the voice of reason in the midst of my chaotic mind and sometimes emotional break downs. He was a realist but faithful and positive at the same time. Although I think he was trying to protect me from his fears, that surfaced every now and then. He loved being a father. Alexis had become the light of his life. He was a different guy with her. He never once doubted that we would lose our daughter. His faith helped me believe that everything was going to be alright. I trusted his faith more than I depended on my own. He was truly my rock and I was so glad he was going through this with me.

I would like to believe we were there for each other. I tried my best to comfort him when I thought he needed it. For me, comfort was sex. It was the only way I thought we could be close. You couldn't get any closer than sex, besides I wanted him to know that I still loved him no matter what was going on in our lives. Okay, I'll admit sex was as much for me as it was for him, maybe more so. I bet you're thinking who would be thinking about sex while their child was going through so much? Me! Sex made me feel better, not to mention it was fun! It was a momentary escape from reality. New York and I both needed that. Of course, he didn't mind, he was a guy. Why would he? I just think being intimate brought us closer and helped us get through what was happening in our little family. However, I'm sure if you were to ask him he would say I was the one who wanted sex all the time and he was just trying to make me happy.

He may even be right, although he never once put up a fight. Sex with him was love and love is what I wanted to feel instead of all the other junk that was crowding my heart. Making love to him was amazing as always and it always made me feel better. But I wasn't any more careful now than I was before. I knew everything that could and did happen, so you would think I would use a bit more common sense. Nope, and so three months after Alexis was born I was pregnant...again!!

The following months were filled with operations, specialists and doctor's visits from Augusta, Georgia to Charleston, SC. It seemed like there was always somewhere for us to be. New York had to work so most of this traveling fell on my mother. She was great about it. Anytime I needed her, she was right there. Sometimes when we had to be in Charleston, we stayed at the Ronald McDonald House. It was a great help to stay there because everything was free. We also got a chance to meet other families who had children in the hospital. Being with other parents who had sick children made me feel a little less lonely. It was nice to have others to talk to who actually understood what I was feeling, or most of what I was feeling.

I didn't think anyone could understand the tremendous amount of guilt I felt. I blamed myself for what was happening to my baby. It was my fault that she had to endure everything she was facing. I was responsible for the way the world would see her and how people would treat her. Someone somewhere had lied to my mother all those years ago when all the same issues happened to me. Whatever this thing was that came and attacked and tried to destroy my heart and eyes had to be hereditary. How else could it be explained? How could it be twenty years later that my baby ended up almost exactly where I had been, but worse. Needless to say, I did this to my precious baby girl. It was all on me! And now I was gripped with the fear that this nightmare could happen all over again when I gave birth to our second child. I bet none of the parents at the Ronald McDonald House had to carry that around.

It took time for to come to terms with what was happening to my daughter, and what most likely would happen to the new baby. I couldn't wrap my mind around what was happening and why. Of course, I questioned God: I will even go so far as to say I blamed Him. How could I not? In my heart, I believed in Him and with that, I believed He controlled everything. Therefore, He allowed this to happen. So, praying was hard for me, going to church was even harder, and singing was the hardest of all. Singing was a gift from God to me. I felt it was a special thing between Him and me, that thing that got me through some rough times. It's something I shared with others gladly and the one thing I thought I did well. But during this time, I just couldn't sing to God. I felt like He betrayed me in some way. I know it may sound crazy and even a bit selfish considering all the wonderful things He had done for me, especially after all the sinful things I had done. And maybe this was my punishment for every bad thing I had done. Maybe this is what happened when you have sex outside of marriage. Maybe God was tired of the excuses I gave for all the bad choices I made. Maybe my little girl was paying the price for the sins of her mother. All these thoughts and countless more ran through my head all the time. I couldn't find any peace, and I struggled trying to understand. Not to mention, although New York never said it I felt like he blamed me as much as I blamed myself. I needed answers, there had to be someone to blame, if not me then who? I was angry and I needed someone to blame…and so God was it.

Church was the place I ran to feel safe and at peace. And even with everything that was going on between God and me, it was still the place I felt most comfortable. Things were different there now. I can't say that anyone treated us any differently when we came. There was still love and acceptance there, even though we had had a child out of wedlock. I didn't feel judged or looked down upon, it was just different. I was different. Life had happened and it changed me. We were so young, faced with all these grown up decisions and life challenges. It was hard. Church was the place that allowed me to sing the pain away. My voice was my instrument of healing, not just for others but for me as well. But I wasn't singing now. I felt like it would be hypocritical standing before others singing to God all the while knowing what I had done, what I was doing. My heart wasn't right with God, and it didn't take my bishop to tell me that I needed to stop singing. I already knew. I couldn't imagine how he would react when he found out I was pregnant again. I don't even remember when I told him. I just remembered that everything felt off balance. I felt I was falling into a bottomless black hole…all alone.

I tried to be happy about the new baby but the truth is I didn't want another child. I didn't know how to care for the one I had. I was so afraid of doing something wrong or doing too much or not enough. I had help with Alexis, but I still felt alone. The joy that came with having a new baby wasn't there. Don't get me wrong, I was very grateful that my baby was home and doing well. I felt blessed to even be her mother. But mostly, all I ever felt was fear. I was afraid that we were going to have to relive this nightmare all over again with the new baby. I wondered how I was going to take care of two health-challenged children on my own. I already had one visually-impaired daughter, while I was also visually impaired. The thought of doing this again terrified me. Even though anyone else ever said it, I knew they were all thinking the same thing. If it happened once, it could happen again. I know my mother was disappointed in me although she never said so. I know New York was angry with me, although he never said so. It was okay because I was angry enough for everybody. And no one could be more disappointed in me as I was in myself. But I felt the sorriest for this new baby; she had no idea what she was coming into.

The months leading up to the birth of our new addition passed quickly. I was huge with this baby, much bigger than I had been with Alexis. It didn't help that I was eating as often as I possibly could. My food of choice was hotdogs, preferably from Sonic. Oh, they were so good!! I could eat a footlong Coney with no problem. Carrying this baby was real work. I was always tired. And for some reason that I can't recall, I would faint a lot, no warning at all, just drop. I didn't want to go anywhere or do anything, just eat and sleep. Everything and everyone seemed to annoy me. I have heard stories of how mean and irritable I was back then. I remember crying a lot, call it hormones or whatever but I was a mess!! All my friends were off at college having a ball and I was home with one kid and pregnant with another. Not what I had planned! I must have driven my family and friends crazy, especially New York.

We learned early on that we were expecting another girl. This made things easier because we already had everything we needed. However, my family was a little disappointed. Our family was filled with girls. My grandmother had two daughters who had three daughters between them. And I was the mother of two daughters. My little cousin Brian was the only biological man in my grandmother's clan. And of course, New York was hoping for a son so we would have one of each. I personally didn't care; I just wanted a healthy baby. So, when I was far enough along in the pregnancy, my cardiologist suggested I come for an extensive fetal ultrasound.

This ultrasound would be able to see into my baby's heart to determine if there were any defects. And by the grace of God, there were none. We had to wait until she was born to see if there were any problems with her eyes. Time seemed to stand still. My mind filled with all the dreadful possibilities that awaited us in just a few short months.

In the meantime, I tried to focus on all the good things in my life. I had a wonderful guy who seemed to truly love me. My daughter was home with us and was doing well. As far as we knew, there was another healthy baby on the way. My mother and New York had finally reached a place of tolerance and peace. She had grown to love him, which I thought would never happen. We even moved into a new home where we all lived together. Now let me pause right here and say I didn't think this was a good idea. I felt like we needed a home of our own to rear our family. New York felt like we needed my mother's help or maybe he was afraid he couldn't handle everything by himself. Who knows, but I went along with it even though it's not what I wanted. Unpause. Of course, New York and I had separate rooms. It didn't matter, the damage had already been done. It's not like I could get any more pregnant than I already was! Besides we always found time to sneak in a little love making here and there. Things were good.

There was only one thing that would make everything just right, marriage. I had told New York many times that I didn't want to continue to live in sin. I felt we had done enough of that. If we were going to expect good things from God, it was only right that we at least attempt to live right. That may sound crazy to you but, that's how my mind worked. He agreed with me for the most part. I know he wasn't quite ready to seal the deal. To be honest, neither was I, but why not? We had already done everything else so why not make it official, right? So, we eventually got engaged. I would like to offer you more details on the proposal but unfortunately, I don't remember. All I can recall is a small, diamond promise ring followed by bigger diamond ring later. I think it was for my twenty-first birthday. Sad huh? I know! But what I will never forget is that on July 10, 1996, we welcomed a completely healthy Alysha Monee' into the world!!

Chapter Nine
The Family Life

Exactly one month later to the day of Alysha's birth, New York and I tied the knot. We had a simple ceremony on a Friday afternoon at home in our living room. There are no extravagant details to recall or any breathtaking moments that come to mind. Bishop performed the ceremony in front of some family and a few friends. Of course, our beautiful daughters were there to see mommy and daddy make it official. I remember my family and I pulling the wedding together with whatever we could find useful. I had a lot of the "something old" and the only new thing we had new was our daughter Alysha. I used my aunt's old flower bouquets from her wedding. My little cousins were the flower girls; we found flowers for them around the house. I wore my high school graduation dress (Yes, I could still fit it after having two kids) and New York wore one of his favorite pant suits. For some crazy reason I can't recall, I allowed Teddy to give me away. Yea, that Teddy! I have no idea what I was thinking; he was probably the only man available at the time. The ceremony was quick and sweet. Standing next to him, giving my life to him forever was the happiest moment of my life. Yes, I was scared too, but happiness trumped fear. The one moment that stands out in memory for me was the very end of the ceremony. We had already pledged our love, said our vows and all that good stuff; I sang to him "At Last," the one song that summed up everything I was feeling at the time. I didn't get two lines into the song before the tears started flowing like a river. My heart was so full of love and gratitude; this man had just given his life and love to me forever. To me! I never thought anyone would choose me and he did. I couldn't see anything past that moment. I wanted to live right there in that moment forever. But that moment was just that, a moment.

Truth be told neither one of us was ready to get married. Not to say that we weren't planning on it, but not this soon. As much as we loved each other and we did love each other, marriage was a big deal that we hadn't prepared for. We had just barely made it to the other side of our own personal hell. We had to grow up fast after Alexis was born. The stress of all her health issues, operations, and then the birth of another child had forced us to become adults way before we were ready. But there was this unspoken pressure from those on the outside that insisted marriage was the next obvious step and it needed to happen NOW!! You know those unsubtle comments like "Well y'all got them girls, marriage must be next?" or "So I guess y'all will be getting married soon." Some people were more forthcoming and direct and just said, "Y'all need to get married!" Yea, the heat was on us to get this thing done. I must admit I was a part of the pressure band, too. Although I wasn't ready to be a wife, I wanted to be one. I felt like being married guaranteed that New

York would always be there. Not to mention marriage would make me feel less terrible about doing it all out of order in the first place. Needless to say, most of the pressure fell on New York. As far as all were concerned, he was the stranger that moved down here and got this naive little country girl pregnant. So, he just had to marry me. I knew he wasn't ready. But he married me because he did love me and he knew how much I loved him. Besides, according to everyone else it was the right thing to do. And he just wanted to do the right thing.

There was no honeymoon, we just jumped right into married life. I was so happy to be his wife. It gave me a sense of purpose. I wasn't sure what I was going to do with my life after losing my sight. Now my life was full and I didn't have time to do anything else. I was now a wife and mother, which didn't leave room for much else. I enjoyed doing all the wifely things for my new husband. Of course, my favorite was the unlimited guilt-free endless supply of married sex! And no matter what anyone tells you, it is significantly different from any other kind. Now we could have all the sex we wanted without feeling bad about it. Yes, I did feel bad about it before, not enough to stop, but bad nonetheless. Anyways, now it was guilt free, shame- free sex whenever we wanted. And I wanted as much of it as I could get. As you may have already figured out, sex became my favorite pastime once I got past the ugly part. I loved it! So, did he by the way! That was a plus to this married thing. I liked that part the most. I also liked not having to search anymore. I had someone I loved with all my heart who loved me back. I no longer had to put myself out there to get noticed. Neither did I have to allow myself to be used to get someone to like me. I belonged to someone and to me there was no greater feeling. I now had what everyone else was looking for. I had love!

Being a mother didn't come as naturally to me as I thought it would. I had an amazing mother, so I knew exactly what I was supposed to do. All I needed to do was follow her example. I had to make sure to give my girls all my love, which I did. I had to make sure they had what they needed, you know the basics...feed them, change them, play with them, and all that good stuff, which I did. But something was off. I tried very hard but it wasn't as easy as I thought. Let me start by saying I was blessed to have a lot of help. New York was great with the girls. He had to work a lot but when he wasn't working, he was right there with us. My mother still worked a lot, but she came home every day and went into full Nana mode. Alexis still had to see various doctors for regular checkups, and my mother usually took us to those. My grandmother came over every day to help me with the girls, too. So, you would think this motherhood thing would be a piece of cake for me..Nope!

I was overwhelmed having two small children. And even though Alexis was eleven months old, she still was quite the handful. When I tell you, this kid would scream her head off. I mean she could let it rip.

On top of that she would bang her head on the floor, bite the side of her playpen, or whatever it took to drive me insane. But the kicker is, she would only act like that when we were alone. When her daddy or Nana was around, she was the perfect little angel. When Grandma came over, Alexis was the sweetest child. But just as soon as it was just her and me, she transformed into this demon child. When I tell you, this kid nearly literally drove me crazy!! Nothing I did would calm her down, nothing! There were times she would scream so badly that I would just leave her and Alysha in the house. I would just walk out! I figured that would be better than throwing her against the wall and watching her slide down or putting a pillow over her face so the noise would stop. I would be a liar if I say those thoughts never crossed my mind more than once. I cried all the time. I loved her so much, but she made me feel like I was the worst mother in the world. I was convinced that this child hated me, which was fine with me because at that time I didn't like her that much ether.

 Alysha, on the other hand, was quite the opposite of her bratty, older sister. She was an angel, a quiet sweetheart baby. She rarely ever cried unless she was hungry or needed to be changed. She was the cutest, little fat baby you ever did see. She would just sit in her carrier smiling and look around. As a matter of fact, she was such a quiet baby I started to get concerned. I was worried that maybe something was wrong. Maybe she couldn't hear, since she seemed to be so unresponsive to what was going on around her. So of course, we had her checked out and everything was fine. I was so relieved because I just couldn't take it if something was wrong with her. I didn't want her to go through all the things her sister had to endure. And selfishly, I didn't want to go through all those things again either. I still blamed myself for all the health issues Alexis had. With that blame came the notion that I caused those things to happen somehow, which in turn made me determined not to hurt Alysha the same way. I had gotten it in my mind that I could contaminate my baby just by being near her. So, I kept my contact with her to a minimum. I rarely picked her up unless it was necessary. My mother or New York took care of her most times during the night. Grandma was there with me most days, so I usually insisted she hold her or feed and change her. This went on for quite some time. I never told anyone what I was feeling. In my mind, I was doing what I needed to protect her from whatever it was in me that made Alexis so sick. Call me crazy, but I was afraid I was going to break her inside, make her sick some way. I loved her too much to hurt her. I was just trying to be a good mother.

If I am to be completely honest, there was a small part of me that didn't want to connect with Alysha. I was consumed with guilt and fear, but fear more than anything. Not only was I afraid to hurt her, I was also afraid that she would hurt me. Fear led me to believe that if I got too close to her, she would get sick. Then I was afraid that if she got sick, she would die. What were the chances that God would spare both my girls? He could, but would He? I couldn't take that chance. Losing her would destroy me. So, in some strange way, in my mind, protecting her from me also protected me from losing her. I know, it's crazy how my mind worked back then. I was just trying to be a good mother. Needless to say, it took some time for me to bond with my baby.

One day when my grandmother was leaving to go home, she told me she wasn't coming back. "You need to learn how to be a mother to these children," she said. And just like that I was on my own. I was terrified! I didn't know how to do this by myself! I needed her! But, no matter how much I begged her she didn't come back, not to stay anyway. So, there I was with these two little girls, one who couldn't stand me and the other I had no clue how she felt about me. I had to figure this thing out. Many days I cried and cried, but I pulled myself together and get back to it. There were other times when I wallowed in disappointment and self-pity. This was not a part of the plan. I wanted to go back to school and get a job. My mother's voice would echo in my head, "Being a mother is your job." And boy was it ever! There was always something that needed to be done. From diapers to feedings to playing and teaching them, it was a full-time job! I a loved being a mother. I just didn't think I was very good at it. But like they say, "Practice make perfect," and I eventually got the hang of it. I developed a schedule and once I got it perfected, it went smoothly, at least most of the time. I ate when they ate, slept when they slept, and made time each day to teach and play. Being a mom became the most important part of my life.

Being a wife came more easily to me. I'm sure that was because of my mother's example. She was an amazing wife to Teddy, too amazing if you ask me. Anyway, she cooked, cleaned, and took care of everything in the house. So, I just did that. I made sure the house was clean, well as much as it could be, with two little kids running around. We had gotten a nice-sized mobile home with four bedrooms, two and half baths, living and dining room combination, kitchen, laundry area, and den. New York and I had the master suite. Keeping it clean wasn't too difficult, even though he was quite the slob at times. The girls shared a room, which never was that messy. And my mother had her room, which she maintained herself. I made sure everything else was taken care of. I set aside a day each week to do all my household chores. It usually took a while because I would have to stop and do things for the girls, but I got it done. I cooked every day, well mostly every day. I had picked up cooking here and there from my mother and grandmother. I often asked New York what he wanted for dinner each day. I enjoyed doing things for him. I just wanted to make him happy. So being a good wife was extremely important to me. I didn't ever want him to feel he made a mistake in marrying me. I wanted him to feel lucky that he had me. I wanted him to feel he had everything he needed in me. I wanted him to be happy to come home to me each day. My primary focus was to prove my worth to him. I needed him to see me as valuable. I needed to feel valuable. I tried my best to be everything New York wanted and all I thought a good wife should be. I loved him so much. It was truly astonishing that I could love him the way I did. I poured all of myself into this man. That was the only way I knew how to be.

    I knew I could be a handful at times. I didn't mean to be, but I couldn't help it. I loved hard. When I loved someone, I put everything I had into it. I was affectionate, you know kissing and hugging him all the time. I wanted to be with him all the time no matter where he was or what he was doing. I now realize that could be rather smothering, especially if you weren't used to that kind of love. But I didn't know any other way. There were times when I would tell New York how much I loved him that he would just stare at me. I never understood why. I just thought he was taking it all in. I remember him telling me once that I loved him too much. I didn't even think that was possible! Could you love someone too much? It would be times when I got bothered if he didn't express his feelings to me, but I tried not to let it get to me too much. We had those times when I just knew what he was feeling without him saying a word. We laid in bed and talked for hours. He told me stories about his life back in New York and all the things he had done. He had a pretty interesting life. I was always fascinated with his stories. Sometimes I told him stories of what life was like growing up in the south, but my stories were nowhere as good as his.

We had this game we played where I would sit on his back and write messages. He would try to guess what I wrote. Most times, he guessed wrong and we both burst out laughing. We laughed a lot. He always knew how to make me laugh. It was in those midnight moments that I learned that true intimacy went far beyond sex. It was a connection on a deeper level, my husband was truly my best friend.

It's important to note that New York worked just as hard to be a good husband as I did at being a good wife. He was a good guy. He knew there were things that I wanted and he put forth an effort to give them to me. He bought little gifts just because. He went all out for my birthday because he knew my birthday was like my own personal holiday. It wasn't in his nature to just lay his feelings out there, but he did find different ways to express them to me. He often told me what a good person I was or how I had such a big heart. He helped build my confidence by pointing out all the good things about me. He often told me how I was pretty, which I had a real hard time believing. But he saw past the scars in my eyes and the huge glasses, he saw me. Not too many people were able to do that, especially men. He always let me know what a great mother I was exactly when I needed to hear it most. He made it a point to highlight my gifts and talents. For example, he knew singing was a passion of mine, and songwriting had become a part of that passion. He read what I wrote and offered helpful suggestions while encouraging me at the same time. He would take care of the girls while I practiced for hours. And when I sang at church or an event, he always tried to be there to support me. I remember we even talked about having a recording studio one day. He was going to manage me and produce all my music. He wanted to support my dream of being a gospel artist. The fact that my dreams were important to him touched my heart in ways he never knew.

The first couple of years were good and we were happy. New York had taken a better job that required him to work third shift some days. It made it harder for us to spend time together. I would be up with the girls when he came home in the mornings. He would tell me all about his night over breakfast and I would tell him about some little cute thing one of the girls had done. Then he would go to bed. Sometimes, I laid next to him and watched him sleep, just to be with him. Other times, when the girls were napping, I crawled into bed with him for some afternoon love making. We found ways to make it work. He would get up and spend some time with the girls before going back to work at night. He was a great father and those girls loved their daddy. He played tea party with them and let them comb his hair. Sometimes, he was the scary monster chasing them around the house. There were other times when he'd read them books or tell them bedtime stories. We had so much fun together. When he had time off, we took the girls out shopping and to McDonalds. If he had a few days off, we visited out-of-town friends. We tried to spend as much time together as we could, even if we were just at home watching movies. I would say things were good.

    I can only remember loving being married. I loved being a wife and mother. Yes, it took some getting used to but I grew to love it. And as far as I was concerned, this married life was the best life to live. It was hard sometimes and there were times that I felt so overwhelmed, but I was still happy. That all slowly started to change after a few years. I can't say when it all began, maybe it was me. I went through some real rough patches. Sometimes I was sad for no reason at all. Although I loved my life, I wanted more. I felt I was missing something. Something that everyone else had that I didn't, I wasn't sure what it was. I thought if I had a job that would make me feel better. But there weren't too many jobs out there for legally blind people. Not to mention, we couldn't afford to put the girls in daycare. So, I opened my home to other children whose parents couldn't afford daycare either. I didn't charge a lot, just enough to have a little extra money. Taking care of children seemed to be something I was good at, so why not get paid for it? I enjoyed it and it gave me a sense of fulfillment. But, there was still something off.

    I don't know if New York noticed the change in me or not. Maybe he had his own stuff going on, too. He had made friends at his new job, so he had people to hang out with. I think I must have resented him for that because it seemed like I was always left with the girls. Yea, my mother would take care of them if I wanted to go anywhere, but where could I go if there was no one to drive me? Besides, the girls were not her responsibility, they were ours. There were times NY went with his friends and I didn't mind, but I remember this one time when I did. He had told me he was going out but I wanted him to stay home with me. I can't recall why I didn't want him to go, I just didn't. He insisted on going and said he wouldn't be gone long, but I didn't want him to go at all. He went. So, I took his little stuffed tiger and chopped its ears off. I also cut off its whiskers and I think one of its feet. Then, because I knew he would come in the house and go straight to the fridge, I placed the dismembered tiger in a Ziploc bag and put it in the freezer for him to find. Crazy, right? Yea, I know! He was so pissed, needless to say that wasn't the end of it. He took my cabbage patch doll and threw it in a mud puddle! I can honestly say that I was wrong and shouldn't have dismembered his tiger, but in my defense that never would have happened if he had just stayed home!

  We started arguing a lot and I can't even remember what we argued about. It's like we found reasons to pick a fight with each. Thinking back on it now, I have no idea what happened to us. I can't pinpoint a moment when things started falling apart. I just know we were both growing and changing into different people. It's like one day we were happy and the next we weren't. As for me, I wanted more of him. I wanted date nights, weekend getaways, just the two of us. I wanted more than sex, which by the way was never an issue. I wanted affection, hand holding in public, smooches, embraces, and words. I wanted to hear the words, "I love you!" He wasn't saying much at all. There were times when he just shut down. He would just go inside himself and I couldn't reach him. I didn't know what to do when he was like that. I imagined he wanted me to stop smothering him to death. I admit, I was a bit much! But that's okay because someone out there would love to have someone to love them the way I loved him. Now this is where things get a bit hazy. I can't recall the order in which everything fell apart, but I will hit the high pints.

It was the late nineties and the world was introduced to the internet. So, I had to have a Gateway computer. I bet you know where this is going, right? Yep, gateway to trouble! Well, I had discovered a whole new world behind that computer screen. You could talk to people without leaving your house. I was meeting all sorts of people, men and women alike. While he was working, I was left alone. The girls had started school by this time so I had a lot of free time on my hands. Chat rooms, that was where I spent a lot of my free time, meeting people from all over the place. There were all sorts of chat rooms, even a room where they held singing contests. I competed in online singing contests and won a lot of them. Oh, it was so much fun! And it was an escape from my reality, which was not too spectacular at the time. Of course, I told New York all about it and he would warn me to be careful. I didn't pay him much attention at all. I had found something exciting and I became addicted. Whenever I had a free moment, I was in a chat room talking to some new friend I had met. There were times I passed on going out so I could stay home and chat. Yea, I had it bad! Now, I won't go so far as to say that the internet ruined my marriage, but I'm sure it played a part!

Online friendships weren't enough for me. I needed them to be more real, to have an actual relationship with the people I was meeting. So, after some time, and when I felt comfortable enough, I started to give out my phone number. Now, this is when the problem really started. Most of the people I met were men, with a few women mixed in. I didn't give my number to a lot of people, but enough to cause a problem. The crazy part is New York didn't mind at first, not to mention he wasn't aware of certain people I was talking to. I don't think I was trying to hide it. I just didn't see the point in mentioning it. See, I didn't think I was doing anything wrong by talking to these people on the phone from time to time. There were times when he wasn't talking to me so I found someone else to talk to. It became wrong when I started talking to certain people on the phone almost every day, and more of a problem when I started venting all my frustrations and unhappiness. The conversations were innocent enough, nothing inappropriate in my opinion. I was just talking to people. Okay, men, mostly men. Honestly, a couple of men. I liked the attention and the way they seemed to think so much of me. But I will talk more about that later.

This continued for quite some time. My

marriage was changing and I wasn't handling it well. I couldn't understand what was happening to us. We were so in love, so why was it now that he seemed like a stranger to me? We argued over the smallest things, we stopped doing things together, and before I knew it, we were living like roommates. We had even stopped having sex! I knew we were in trouble then because no matter what was happening between us we could always connect in bed. But now that connection was broken; this was bad, really bad! We tried our best to push through it, and we did a pretty good job for a while. But my mother noticed something had changed between us. It was something I didn't feel I could talk to her about. By this time her relationship with New York had strengthened and deepened tremendously. She now loved him like a son. I remember once mentioning to her that I wasn't happy and wanted out of the marriage. She told me if I wanted to leave, I should leave. Can you believe that? I was her daughter and she told me to leave! To say I was shocked is an understatement, but that's just how much she had grown to care about him. I was truly lost during this time so I continued to lose myself online. It was like a whole other world where everything I was dealing with was a small dot compared to everything else. I felt like a different person online, a happier version of me. So, I spent more time online and less time facing the reality that my marriage was falling apart.

    I remember the exact moment I knew my marriage was over. It was a few months after New

York's mother passed from cancer. It was a devastating time for all of us, but more so for him. He and his mother were extremely close and losing her broke his heart; it changed him. I had only seen him this broken one other time in our relationship and that was the day we found out how sick our daughter was. He didn't talk much about how losing his mother had impacted him. He would just sit quietly a lot, more than usual. I can even go so far as to say he shut down. He wouldn't let me get close to him. I had no choice but to stand back and watch him suffer his way through that pain. I felt so incredibly helpless. I still loved him so very much. It broke my heart to see him in so much pain, but there was nothing I could do.

One day he came to me and said, "I don't think I want to be married anymore." Those words pierced me like a million knives in my soul. There are no words to express the depths of that pain. Although he said, "I don't think I want to be married anymore." I heard "I don't love you anymore." Yes, I know exactly what he said and I can even say I understood why he said it in that moment. But I heard something totally different. I heard rejection. I heard, "I don't want you." I heard, "You're not good enough." I heard, "I don't need you." And it was in that moment that I shut down. I put a steel trapped door around my heart and I wasn't letting him back in there no matter how hard he tried. And he did try. He came back and explained how he didn't mean it and he was just hurting. But I wasn't hearing any of that. As far as I was concerned, I was done! The marriage was over and I wanted out! If he didn't want *me*, then I didn't want him either!

For almost a year afterwards, we lived in our home as strangers. He went to work and did whatever it was he was doing. I continued taking care of our kids and our home as I had done before. I shut myself off completely. I didn't want to be touched, held, no affection whatsoever, and absolutely no sex. I was so hurt and so broken, but I never let him see what this was doing to me. I hid all my feelings from him. I found someone else to confide in, to share my pain with. Was I wrong? Yes, I was, but I no longer cared. I still needed someone and if it wasn't going to be him, it was going to be somebody. I had a couple of guys that I talked to regularly to fill the void. See, I was the type of girl who needed attention. I needed to feel wanted and desired. I needed affirmation on a regular basis. I had girlfriends I could talk to, but I preferred my male friends. It was something about a guy who would tell me I was pretty or sexy, or I had a beautiful voice, or I was a good person. I liked positive words from people, but I preferred them from a man. I think this is where my daddy issues kicked in. Afterall, I'd been rejected by my father, step father, and now my husband. Yep, I was seriously messed up and I knew it. I just didn't know how to fix it though. New York stayed until November of 2000, and just like, that my marriage was over.

Chapter Ten
Generations

Sometimes when life happens we may find ourselves in unfamiliar territory, not knowing what to do or how to navigate through it. At least that's how I felt, and for me, I was desperately searching within myself for reasons. What did I do wrong? What could I have done differently or better? I know it takes two people to make a marriage succeed or fail, but I took my inability to save my marriage personally. I felt like a failure. The one thing I thought I would do well (being a wife) had proven to be the one thing I had completely screwed up. I can now admit that I could have fought harder to save my marriage, but I had my reasons for not doing so. I will talk about them a little later. My marriage was over! There was no coming back for New York and me; it was truly and completely finished for us. I had now placed my daughters in the very situation I was so desperately trying to avoid, a home without a father. Thinking back on it, that's all I had ever seen in my immediate family…homes without fathers. This new unfamiliar place that I now found myself was not so new to the women closest to me. It went back generations.

It started as far back as I can remember. The fathers of the children in our immediate family were missing, either through death, abandonment, or we simply left them. Let's start with my great grandmother East. I don't know much about her, only the things I was told. She had been raped by a white man who is the father of her oldest son. So, I'm quite sure he didn't play the role as father to her son. She later married my great grandfather and had four more children. My great grandfather died when my grandmother Mary was very young. No one seems to know much about him or the circumstances surrounding his untimely death. So, she was left to raise her five children alone. She never remarried. As a matter of fact, I was told that she was never seen with another man after her husband died. Not to say that she may not have had one stashed away somewhere, but it seemed highly unlikely. All I can ever remember hearing about her is that she loved God, loved her children and she took care of them the best she could during those times. She was a strict disciplinarian who didn't tolerate disrespect or disobedience. My mother told me that my great grandmother was the strongest woman she has ever known. And as far as I know, she was the first woman in our family to raise her children without a father.

Then there was my grandmother, who also got married and had two daughters of her own. I mentioned earlier how she left her husband in Virginia and moved back to South Carolina with her children. All she ever told me is that she didn't like living in Virginia and she wanted to move back. My grandfather didn't want to leave, so she left without him. It was also rumored that my grandfather was being unfaithful, so maybe that played a part in her wanting to leave. In any case, she left him! She didn't even bother to get a divorce, so they're still married to this very day! Although my grandmother had dated plenty men throughout the years, my mother and my auntie grew up without their father. Yes, they knew him but he never played an active role in their lives, neither physically or financially.

So that leaves my mother and my auntie. Auntie got married and had one son and two daughters. I don't know how long she was married, neither will I get into all the issues and circumstances within the marriage. I honestly don't know all the details, but what I do know is that eventually the marriage ended. She moved back to South Carolina from Florida with her three children. She worked and took care of them by herself with no financial support from their father. However, he did make it a point to come visit here and there, and my little cousins went to stay with him during most summers. My cousins had some sort of working relationship with their father. Not to mention, after some years my auntie remarried and there was a strong father presence in their home. But the fact remains that their biological father wasn't in their home nor did he have a major role in their lives.

That leaves my mother, and I have already shared that story. My father wasn't there and my step father wasn't too interested in taking his place. So, where does that leave us? A family of very strong independent women raising children without the help of the men who created them. Do you see the pattern tracing all the way back to my great grandmother? And now I am one of them. I was now faced with raising my girls without their father in the home. This isn't what I planned. This isn't what I wanted for them. One of the main reasons I wanted to be married is so that my daughters would have their father. And I dropped the ball! He was gone from our home, but that didn't mean he couldn't be a great father, right? Wrong! But that's another story for another time.

    I strongly believed in generational curses and it appeared to me that we were cursed. All the women in my family had pretty much ended up in the same situation. What I couldn't understand is why? I thought I would be the one to break the three-generation curse, but instead I added to it. I was devastated, not so much for me but for my children. I knew what it felt like to long for a father that wasn't there. I knew the pain of seeing other daughters with their fathers and wishing to be them. I knew the gigantic hole my father had left in my heart. And I also knew the crazy things I had done to try and fill it. My father's absence had turned me into someone I didn't want to be. I didn't like who I had become and all the choices I had made because of it. I didn't like the insecurity I carried or the low self-esteem I tried to hide. More than anything I absolutely hated loving a father so much who didn't even care that I existed. I wanted to protect my daughters from my reality, from walking out all my mistakes. I wanted to protect them from the pain and rejection that was sure to come from their father not being in their lives. And in all my efforts to protect them, I failed.

God the Father

This family of women I grew up in was a strong one. And no matter what trials they've had to endure, their strength and faith was deeply rooted in their relationship with God. Although each had their unique way of relating to Him, maybe some closer, essentially God was the core of it all. Every good thing was a gift from God. And every bad thing, if God brought you to it He will take you through it. That was the basis of how the women lived in my family as far back as I can remember. That faith was then passed on to me. God was all we needed. He was the man in our lives. From the time I was a small child, I was taught that God was the source of absolutely everything. God was our Father.

For me, the concept of God was harder to grasp at first. So, you're telling me God concreated the whole earth, everything and everyone in it by Himself, right? Okay! And not only that, He's this enormous larger- than-life invisible being that lived passed the clouds somewhere. And I was supposed to also believe He was my father, too? That's a bit much for a little kid to take it, don'tcha think? I know some adults who still can't wrap their heads around that one. Not to mention if God was my father, how could He be everyone else's father, too? Besides I was selfish! If He was going to be my father, I didn't want to share Him with anyone else. It took some convincing, but over time it eventually soaked in. But, there was just one question that everyone else had. If God made the world and everything in it, then who made God? Right?

My mother made sure that I went to church, if not with her, then with one of our neighbors. I've had plenty of preachers and teachers attempt to answer that one burning question. But no one could tell me where God came from. "He just is!" was usually the response given by everyone I asked. It became quite clear to me that no one knew the answer, though some tried hard to explain it to me. So, I learned how to just go with that. Then there was heaven, hell, angels, satan, and of course Jesus. It was a lot to wrap my mind around and boy did I try. Eventually, it became less important to understand how it all worked, but more to just believe that it did. For a while I felt I didn't have a choice in the matter. It was like I inherited God like one would inherit brown eyes or dimples. I had to believe in God because my mother said so, although she never actually said those words.

As the years passed I had opportunities to experience God for myself. So many times, in my life things happened that couldn't be explained by anything other than God. I finally put it all together in my mind and heart in a way that made sense to me. It all boiled down to faith. The ability to have complete trust or confidence in something, in this case someone that I couldn't see. Faith had most definitely become a huge part of my life, and it worked for me. And although I didn't have all the answers and can't explain it in a way that others might get it, I knew God existed.

I eventually got to a place where my relationship with God was vital in my life. But to be honest, it wasn't a consistent one. I trusted and believed in Him, or at least I tried. But there were times when I put Him aside. Sometimes I did things that I knew I shouldn't have. Other times, I made decisions based on whatever selfish desire I had at the moment. I wasn't always honest. I wasn't always good. I certainly didn't keep all the commandments, and there were times I am sure I disobeyed Him altogether. When things were bad, or I was hurt, angry or in my feelings about one thing or another, I was quick to blame him. And when things were good, I didn't always acknowledge Him or show gratitude. To sum it all up, I wasn't the best Christian at all. But who is? What I can say is no matter what I did, I always came back to Him. I kept trying to get it right because I didn't want a life without Him.

Faith in God was the one thing that bonded our family together. It was the one thing that we all had in common. No matter where we were in our lives or what happened in our lives, God is who got us through it all. We prayed together. We believed together. God truly was the father of our family passed from one generation to another.

Chapter Eleven
The Lost Years

I'm going to try not to confuse you as I dive into all the events that occurred after New York and I separated. I'm relatively sure the sequence of events may not be written in the exact order in which they occurred; however, they are all true. Truth is, this was a very confusing time for me. I was utterly and completely lost. I had so many different emotions running through me. I was disappointed, angry, and hurt, just to list a few of my emotions. I was hurt because I truly loved this man with all my heart and now he was gone. But the crazy part is I didn't want him to come back. I had made a vow to myself when I was a little girl that if I ever got married and it came a time that I wasn't happy that I would end it. As much as I wanted a father in the home for my children, I wasn't willing to sacrifice my own happiness to give them that. Call me selfish, but I wasn't prepared to be unhappy and expose my children to an unhappy home just to be able to say their father was there. I had been the child in that situation and it had broken me in ways my mother never knew. I had witnessed the arguments and fights between her and Teddy. I had seen her tears and I knew she wasn't happy, yet she stayed. I suppose she had her reasons for that, but as for me I wasn't going to do that to my children no matter what. I believed that New York wasn't happy either and wanted to leave long before he ever spoke the words out loud. I refused to let either of us be held hostage in an unhappy marriage, so I let go. And that's why I didn't fight to save my marriage, no one wanted to save it. But letting go was one of the most painful things I ever had to do.

There was an emptiness when New York left. I didn't know who I was now that I wasn't his wife. So much of me was wrapped up in him and his love for me. I had truly lost myself, not knowing who I was to start with. The girls were in school by then and I was left home all day every day with no one to take care of. I had no clue what to do next. I had settled on the reality of being wife and mother; that was my job and I grew to love it. But now I didn't know what I was supposed to do. Yes, I still had my girls to take care of, but they didn't need me as much now that they were older. Everything I had worked so hard to build had fallen apart. All the choices I made led to this. I felt numb; I knew this was happening but it didn't feel real. I felt I was watching someone else's life fall apart but I was powerless to help them. But that someone was me! I felt so alone. I didn't know who I could turn to. I didn't know anyone my age who had gone through this and come out on the other side. And the one person who did know exactly what I was going through was my best friend who just happened to be my husband, the one person I could no longer run to. Lost! I was completely lost!

It was two years before New York and I finalized our divorce. During this time, I tried to redirect my focus off all my emotions and unto my girls. I knew I would eventually get myself together. Of course, my children were priority. I wanted to do whatever I could to make sure they were happy. They had a hard time after their father left, especially Alexis. She was most definitely a daddy's girl. She cried for him all the time. Although he came to see them often and took them over the weekend, that wasn't enough for her. She wanted her daddy with her all the time. She didn't understand or accept that he was no longer living in our house. She often came home from school expecting to find him and cried when he wasn't there. School was difficult for her due to her issues with her vision. She needed a lot of extra help with homework, things such as reading and writing. She wanted her daddy's help, not mine. She wanted daddy to get her a snack, daddy to read her a story and daddy to tuck her in at night. It was things like those which made his absence so much harder to bare.

    Alysha, on the other hand, seemed to process things a bit differently. She clung to me more. Wherever I was, there she was. It was like she could sense that I needed something, and in her little four-year old mind she became responsible for making sure I was alright. She offered to sleep with me almost every night. Maybe she thought I was lonely. She told me how much she loved me all the time. It was so cute, looking into her little face seeing her smile up at me. There was so much love in her eyes, and I needed that. She did whatever she could to make sure that her big sister didn't miss her daddy too much. I watched her change into such a serious little person, always trying to make sure we were okay. I t was a process for all of us, but we eventually made our way to a new normal.

It seemed to me as soon as I got used to the fact that New York and I were over, I had to accept the fact that he had moved on to someone else. Now that was very hard to swallow. I knew the time would come when both of us were going to find someone else, yet he discovered someone a lot sooner than I anticipated. I wasn't ready to accept another woman with my husband. We weren't even divorced yet, and there he was bringing another woman to OUR home to pick up OUR children! To say I was upset is an understatement. I was furious! All sorts of thoughts ran through my mind, but the one that rang like a clanging cymbal was, "He cheated on me!" As far as I was concerned, there was no other explanation to why this was happening so soon after we split. Where did this chic come from? I didn't care what he said or how he tried to explain it away. My mind was made up; he had betrayed me and I didn't know how I was going to get past that.

It wasn't even that he found another woman. I didn't care about that part. I was more focused on *when* and *why* he chose another woman. See, I expected him to be alone for a while, grieve our relationship, you know focus on bettering himself and being a good father. What I did not expect was for him to forget me so easily and move on so quickly, as if I never existed. Maybe that wasn't his thought process at all, but all I felt was betrayal and rejection. How could this man who I brought to my town leave the life we spent almost six years building just move on? Where did all his love go? Did he ever even love me? What about everything we had been through? What about our children? What about me? Was I so easily replaceable? Apparently so, and I didn't understand. It didn't make sense to me. Then I thought about it, this new woman was everything I wasn't. I was a legally blind, unemployed, college dropout who couldn't drive with absolutely nothing to offer but our two children and all the love I had given. That wasn't enough, and neither was I.

Hatred had begun to slowly inch its way into my soul. It was the kind of feeling I had never felt before. It was a silent but all-consuming disdain for him. I couldn't stand the sight of him or bare the mention of his name. Every time I thought of him, anger would rise in me until I could barely focus on anything. Up until this point, there were people that I strongly disliked but never had I experienced this type of feeling. I did my best to hide it, and for the most part not too many people noticed. I prayed hard and often until I just couldn't pray anymore. I tried to push the feeling down but little things brought it to the surface. Like the fact that New York rarely gave me any money to help take care of the girls. Or how he wasn't there for all the hard stuff that I had to deal with concerning our children. Or when he said he was coming to get them but didn't for whatever reason. Or when he did show up, he thought it was just fine to bring that woman to my house! Every time he hurt me, the more the hatred grew.

The pain wasn't as easy to hide. My mother could see how much it hurt me to see how he was moving on with someone else. This was one of those times that there was nothing she could say or do to fix it for me. But that didn't stop her from trying. She called and cursed them both out for being inconsiderate and disrespectful, but that only made things worse for me. It made me appear weak, as if I was helpless and incapable of defending myself. Maybe it was true because I never said a word to New York about how I was feeling. I wasn't going to give him the satisfaction of knowing he hurt me so badly. He never knew what was growing inside of me. I didn't even grasp how my emotions were taking a toll on me. I remember the first time I saw her sitting in the front seat of his car from my bedroom window. She sat there waiting for him to return with my children. It hurt watching them drive away like they were a family. This woman had taken the place that used to be mine; she now had my family. There was an indescribable ache that made my entire body tremble. After all I had been through, that moment was the greatest pain I had ever known. And all I wanted was for it to stop.

This was the first time in my life when I wanted to die. It was the strangest feeling, this tremendous sense of loss and despair. I felt like there was no reason for me to be alive. I didn't want to be alive. I wasn't thinking of my children or my mother or anyone else for that matter. I just wanted to disappear. I walked into my bathroom and looked for anything that would help me do just that. All I found was a bottle of Benadryl and so I took as many as I could swallow, handful after handful. I don't even know how many it was, but I remember it was a lot. I recall lying in bed, saying a quick prayer, and crying myself to sleep. The plan was to hopefully wake up in heaven; I wasn't sure if that would happen but at that time I was willing to take the risk anyway. I honestly don't know for sure how God and suicide work, the jury is still out on that one as far as I'm concerned. I just hoped He would have mercy on pitiful me. In any case, it didn't matter because I woke up the next morning in my bedroom. Call me crazy, but I was very disappointed in the outcome. I was still in pain, extremely drowsy, and with a major headache. You would think I'd be grateful to still be alive but instead I felt like a failure; suicide was just another thing I had failed at.

The Boys

Little Boy

Have you ever done something so incredibly stupid that you vowed to never tell anybody? I did! My encounter with Little Boy is what I refer to as my "Dirty little secret." There is only one other person who knows what happened between us, but now everyone will know. I initially decided not to include him in my story, but soon realized it was too important to omit. He was the beginning of my downward spiral into self-destruction. There's not too much to say about him being that I barely knew him, other than the fact that he was little. He was short and skinny, no one that I would have ever dated or been attracted to. Anyway, we started talking on the phone after I had met him online a month or so before. He was very straight forward with what he wanted, sex! Now for some reason knowing this didn't deter me from talking to him. I was more curious than anything. Why would a married man be looking for sex?

I knew it was a bad idea from the start, but that didn't stop me from walking right into a mess. I think I figured it was harmless to flirt with him over the phone, since the chances of me seeing him were slim to none. I can't quite remember where he stayed, but I do recall it was far enough away. I was flattered by all his compliments and turned on by all his seductive talk. But as I said, I thought nothing of it. I just liked the attention, and at that point I was taking all the attention I could get. I wasn't too picky about who gave it to me. I did kind of feel bad because he was married, but at the same time so was I. Honestly, I didn't care. Soon enough he asked to come see me and I told him he could. The thing is I didn't believe he would, but he showed me.

He called me one afternoon and told me he would be in McCormick in an hour or so. I was shocked, but I told him I would meet him at a friend's house. He showed up, we had very bad sex, and then he left. It happened just like that. I didn't leave anything out. The whole meet, greet, and sex lasted all of forty-five minutes. It was terrible! I couldn't believe that I had just had the worse sex ever with a married stranger. But I did and I wasn't even sure why I did it. I could have very easily said no, but for some reason I went right along with it like it was my duty. Part of it was so I wouldn't be considered a tease, I had done my fair share of seductive talk, too. I didn't want him to be mad having driven all that way for nothing. You know? The other part was I wanted to see if he was good as he said he was. He was not!! He was one major disappointment and a wasted sin! It didn't make sense to me then and it makes even less sense to me now. I felt so dirty, nasty and bad. It was so out of character for me to do something like that. I didn't know what was happening to me. I didn't feel badly for too long. I just buried it deep in the back of my mind, and I never spoke to him after that. All I know is if I could take back anything, that would be it.

Big Boy

Big Boy was one of the first guys I started chatting with online. We got to be pretty, good friends. He was there when things started to fall apart in my marriage. He encouraged me to try hard and work things out. It was nice having someone to talk things out with; he was like the voice of reason. Even after New York moved out, he was still telling me to have hope that things would work themselves out. But I knew that wasn't going to happen. Big Boy and I talked almost every day, sometimes in chat rooms but mostly on the phone. It was crazy how we just seemed to click like we had known each other for years. He became a very important part of my life. And the best part is he didn't want anything from me. He was just satisfied with the friendship, which was good because friendship was all I could handle at the time. I was not in any way ready to start a new relationship with anyone. I can't speak for him but I had grown to care about him. So, I figured meeting in person was the obvious next step. This is when things got interesting.

We had exchanged pictures when we first started chatting. He often complimented me on how pretty he thought I was. I still needed to hear that kind of stuff. He was a nice-looking guy too, well at least based on the picture he sent me. Turns out he had sent me a picture of someone else. I am not even sure why he did that. Maybe he thought it would change things between us if I knew what he looked like. But when he realized I was coming to visit, he was forced to tell me the truth. When I received the picture of what he looked like, I was completely blown away. It wasn't that he was ugly or anything like that. He was quite handsome; there was just a lot more of him than he had led me to believe. I didn't care that he was a, "BIG BOY," he was still the same person on the inside, which is all that mattered to me. So, I was "catfished" before catfishing was even a thing.

A friend and I drove over three hours to meet Big Boy. I was so excited to meet him, to finally see him face-to-face. He had become such a great friend and I was just looking forward to hanging out with him, no strings attached. Everything went fine; he was just as excited to see me as I was to see him. We went out, grabbed some food and went back to my room to catch up. Okay, well then things took an unexpected turn. I was under the impression that we were just friends, although we had flirted with each other a little bit, I didn't think it meant anything. I was obviously mistaken! Things got rather heated in that hotel room. We didn't have sex but we sure did come close enough. Too close for me, but I did nothing to stop it. I liked the way he made me feel while touching me. I enjoyed the closeness, being held by him. I didn't realize how much I missed that. It had been a long time since I had felt so safe and loved. I don't know why I allowed myself to be put in that position. I guess I still needed to feel like someone wanted me, even if it was just for a night. I wasn't expecting it; I really wasn't but once I was in the moment I just went with it.

The next day, it was if nothing had happened the night before. We hung out for a while and then said our goodbyes. I remember right before I left to go home, he told me he loved me. I knew exactly what those words meant, and I was fine with it. Oddly enough I loved him too, very much actually, but not in a romantic way but as a special person in my life. The strange thing about all of this for me was that something had shifted in me. I felt different. I didn't want to be with him, neither did I desperately want him to want me. I was good with the night we spent together and very relieved that he didn't try to turn it into anything other than what it was. Both of us needed something and we found it in each other in that time we spent together. And that was that. I went home and we continued to be friends for a long time. And I was good with that.

Baby Boy

I can't even explain how I got entangled in this situation. All I can say is that I was trying to be a listening ear to someone who I thought needed it. It turned out to be way more than I bargained for. And yes, I met this one online too! This young man was extremely intelligent, good looking, and as you may have guessed, way younger than me. Don't worry about how young, that's not important for the story. Well maybe it is, nevertheless I won't reveal his age at the time. Anyway, this guy was a charmer and to say he was troubled is an understatement. Either way, I was an idiot! So, he had a lot of family drama going on. I mean a lot, but I won't go into all that. Even after all these years, I wouldn't betray him by airing his dirty laundry. I found myself caught up in his life and all the drama therein. He was needy, always needing something from me whether it be my time, affirmation and eventually my money. The crazy part is how I bent over backwards trying to give him what he asked for, whatever it was. As if I wasn't needed enough by my own children, I had to go and add another *child* to the mix.

The thing is I liked being needed by him. As a matter of fact, it gave me a new sense of purpose and power…knowing that he needed me, and I got to choose whether to be available or not. I usually made myself available to him because he became angry when I didn't. He threw these temper tantrums, just like a child who was trying to get his way. And me, being the fool that I was always caved to him. I mean I was sending money, staying on the phone all hours of the night, searching for stuff for him online, and whatever else he needed. He even asked me to buy him a laptop once. I refused to do that; my stupid didn't go that far. We argued about silly things I can't even remember now, and he would hang up on me. Sometimes he wouldn't call for days or answer any of my messages online when he was having one of his little fits. And I worried that I would never hear from him again. I walked around sad and hurt and no one ever knew why. I hated when he was mad at me and he knew it, so he called himself punishing me by not talking to me. And it worked. I didn't even know why this guy had such a hold on me. I didn't know why I let him treat me so badly. He had absolutely nothing to offer me, nothing at all! Yet and still, I fell into this dysfunctional cycle of craziness with him for a long time. And get this, we hadn't even met yet!

We eventually met. I can't remember why we even wanted to see each other. There was no chance of us being in a relationship. There was no chance of us having sex, although I had thought about it several times. But I figured sex would only add to the craziness, and I didn't need to be any more of a fool than I already was. There was nothing beneficial about him being in my life. He had brought me way more drama than I needed. But, I still wanted to see him. He made the long drive to South Carolina to see me. When he finally arrived, it was the most awkward first meeting ever. We barely spoke and there was no excitement at all. The entire weekend was uncomfortable. He acted as if he didn't want to be there, and I was ready for him to leave as soon as he got here.

    The only interesting part of the visit was me having my first joint. I think I only tried it because there was no other way to escape, so why not get high? Well I didn't get high; I only got a headache and a huge appetite. I can laugh when I think about it all now, but at the time it wasn't very funny. I had invited this young, impressionable guy into my life, and I should have been setting a good, Godly example for him. Instead I was also needy, desperately lonely, and extremely broken, so much so that I allowed him to play on all my emotions. I convinced myself that he was in love with me. I needed him to want me, to need me and I don't know why. Truth is, he didn't care about me at all. He didn't even like me. He was only using me and I let him because I cared about him so much. I wanted to help him, rescue him from all the terrible things he was going through. I was a mess, and it took him going to jail for me to let go.

Soldier Boy

He was a different kind of guy, an unexpected surprise. I can't remember when we met, but as you may have already noticed there's a developing pattern. I met him online, too. As time passed, I spent more and more time online, so I was meeting more and more people. Some of them I clicked with and others not so much. But for the ones I met, Soldier Boy left a lasting impression.

Soldier was not a boy at all, he was most definitely a man. He had a great career with the military, his own place, and he had plans for his future. He wasn't easily swayed from his morals, beliefs or opinions about things. He was hands down the most honest and outspoken person I have ever met. He always told me the truth and could care less if it hurt my feelings. He was careful not to hurt my feelings on purpose, but he never sugarcoated anything to spare them either. We talked for hours about anything or nothing, either way the conversation was always interesting. I never knew when he was going to call because he worked a lot but when he promised to call, he usually did. Our relationship was different from any other I had in my life at the time. I never had to figure out what was happening between us because I was clear on what was happening. He showed me the upmost respect, no nasty guy talk or shameless attempts to win my heart to get in my pants. He was the *real* deal.

We talked on the phone for a few months before

we decided to meet. There was no pressure on either side, we just enjoyed talking to each other and wanted to try it in person. I was so nervous to meet him. From where I was sitting, he had all his stuff together and I didn't. I didn't think I deserved him, not even as a friend. I felt I didn't measure up, less than what he needed or deserved. I was quite intimidated by him, although he was a down to earth type of guy. So, he drove up to see me. Our first meeting was great. It was just as it was over the phone, except now it was now face-to-face. Did I mention he was gorgeous? He was GORGEOUS!!! Not too tall but dark, handsome, and built like a brick wall. He gave the best hugs, the kind of hugs that you just melt into and didn't want to let go of. I enjoyed every minute of my time with him.

I was invited to go to wedding in the town where he was stationed. I asked him to meet me there, as my date. I just knew he was going to say "no" but he totally shocked me by agreeing to meet me there. I was freaked out! I didn't know what I was going to wear, how to style my hair, or any of those girly things you're supposed to know for a first date. It had been so long since I had been out on a date. Well, I couldn't recall going out on a real date. I was confused because maybe this wasn't a date at all and I was making more of it than I should have. It felt like a date though and if it wasn't to him, it most definitely was to me. I was so excited I could hardly contain myself. I was also very nervous because we had decided that I was spending the night at his house after the reception. It was a lot of pressure on me. I hadn't stayed with another man since my husband (No, Big Boy didn't count). I didn't know what was going to happen, but I knew what could happen, and I was sure my mind and body wasn't prepared for that.

    I just want to say without going into extreme detail, that it was the best first overnight date ever! He was such a gentleman. If you didn't know us, you would think we had been dating a long time. He was the pull out your chair, "Yes sweetheart" kind of guy. I hadn't felt that special since my Paramedic. He made me feel like the world revolved around me! I had his undivided attention. It was amazing! But even in those moments, I felt so unworthy. It was like I was waiting for someone to wake me up from a beautiful dream. I couldn't fathom why this wonderful man had chosen an unemployed, divorced, legally-blind mother of two. He could have chosen so much better. I was sitting in his home trying to figure out how I got there and why I deserved to be there. But he just had a way of making all the negative self-talk fade away. We had a beautiful night together. The sex was incredible; the best I had EVER had. It came naturally, nothing that was pressured or forced; it was a beautiful experience. And of all the things I had to feel guilty about, giving myself to Soldier wasn't one of them.

    After some time passed, I decided it was safe to introduce him to my girls. He was going to be coming around more so it was important to me that they knew who he was. It's important to note that we were never in a committed relationship. He was clear from the start that he wasn't ready to settle down. I knew he had other women that he shared his time with. I was fine with that. Besides, I was still married. I wanted someone to share my life with again, but I knew I wasn't ready. I didn't want to give my heart to anyone. Not to mention, I was now a packaged deal, and I had to protect my girls. The thing about Soldier was that he *treated* me like a girlfriend. When we were together, he was committed to me. He didn't talk to other women on the phone or acknowledge them when they tried to get his attention. When we went out, he insisted on paying, always opened doors, holding my hand, or putting his arm around me. He often told me I was his girlfriend when we were together and we weren't all bets were off. I was good with that. He took care of the girls and me without my even asking. If I needed him, he did his best to make himself available. If there was something I needed, all I had to do was ask. Perfect guy! We were extremely close, and although it would have been easy to blur the lines, I never did. Don't get me wrong, I loved him very much, probably more than I should have. I refused to fall; I had no intentions of getting my heart involved. But if I had to choose a guy, he would have been that guy. I knew he didn't see me that way. He didn't want a readymade family and although it stung a little, I understood that. One day, he said something to me that no guy had ever said or has said since. He told me he cared too much about me for us to keep having sex. He said he didn't want the sex to ruin our relationship. And as much as I appreciated him respecting me so much, I wasn't going to give up the great sex. I was fine with things the way they were, but he insisted that sex would one day destroy what we had. So, just like that, the amazing, extraordinary sex was over! Turns out, it was the best choice we could have made because we are still friends to this very day.

Pretty Boy

Yes, I met him online. But he wasn't my type and I definitely wasn't his. He was the type of guy who dated the light-skinned, long-hair, model looking girls. I didn't fit into any of those categories. But somehow, we became friends. It was the strangest thing because we did connect deeply on other levels. You would have thought we complemented each other well. I just wasn't in a place to fool myself into thinking he would be with a girl like me. There was no chance of us being together. And I wasn't being negative or anything, it was just a fact. I never attracted guys like him.

I went to see him because I just wanted to meet my friend. I didn't have any expectations at all. I already knew where we stood and we were both on the same page. I knew I wasn't in danger of having sex with him because he didn't see me that way. But what I didn't count on was how my body would react to him. This guy was sexy; oooweeee, he was so sexy! He had an amazing body, even with one eye, I could tell he worked out. His eyes were deep brown with beautiful white teeth; he was pretty! And although I didn't have plans to sleep with him, I sure wanted to. But I didn't, not from the lack of trying though. He just didn't pick up on any of my signals. In any case, we had a nice first visit and it was a bit awkward because I don't think he knew what to do. Honestly, I think he was disappointed upon meeting me.

The one thing that stands out in my mind when I think of him is how I felt like no one would ever love me again. He never knew it, but his actions made me feel like I wasn't pretty enough for him or anyone else for that matter. Maybe he was just being respectful, but other than a short, extremely uncomfortable pity massage, he showed no interest in me at all. You would have thought it didn't make a difference because he wasn't my type anyway, but it did. See, I was attracted to him and would have had no problem having sex with him, but he didn't even want sex from me. Yea, I know, I was all messed up. But sex had become this thing I did whenever I wanted to feel desired or loved. I had gotten to a place where sex didn't hold as much value to me as it had before. All I wanted was for him to want me, but he didn't.

He later started dating this girl who met his criteria. I didn't like it at all. Even though I didn't want to date him, it hurt seeing him date this girl. She was everything that I wasn't and it made me feel small…insignificant. His dating her only confirmed every negative thing I was feeling about myself. It was hard to watch, but I did. I put all my feelings aside to be a good, supportive friend. We continued to be friends, great friends actually, and as a matter of fact, we still are. Guess it's a good thing we never had sex because if we had, he wouldn't be my friend today.

This was just the beginning of the downward spiral I found myself in. No one even knew what was going on inside of me, I didn't even see all the emotional destruction coming. I don't know why I didn't do the "normal" thing after my separation. I should have focused on rearing my children and finding out who I was without New York. I should have given my heart time to heal, so many should haves. But instead, I took a whole different approach to what was happening. I can't even say it was planned, it just happened. I found myself searching again, for something or someone to fill the emptiness. This search led me to parts of myself that I never knew existed.

Chapter Twelve
Lost…

It took some time, but eventually I attempted to get myself together. I learned how to push through the pain and bury my emotions. I got better at hiding my true feelings, so much so that it appeared that I was doing just fine. And that's exactly what I wanted people to see, because I didn't want anyone to know how broken I truly was. I had a couple of people in my life that I could confide in, but even they didn't know everything I was feeling. I learned how to pour myself into other things, I even went back to college. Going to school was something I needed to do for me, it was important to me to finish what I had started. There was still this part of me that wanted to be someone with a job providing for my girls. Also, I wanted to prove that I was capable of success even without my vision or my husband. School also gave me a chance to socialize and meet new people in the real world. See, I still spent a lot of time online; it was so easy to get lost out there in internet land. I figured it was time to change that. After my mom remarried, the girls and I moved to Greenwood, SC. There were better educational opportunities for both girls, but especially Alexis. Also, it was a fresh start in our own little apartment away from all the memories that lived in that house. This was the first time I was on my own.

The taste of freedom was oh so sweet, and

although I had a taste of it before, it was never like this. Now that I had my own place, I didn't have to sneak around to meet guys or have them sneak to see me. I could see whoever I wanted whenever I wanted. However, I was very careful of who I allowed to come to my home. And I made sure not to bring just anyone around my girls. So, most of my visitors came around late at night after the girls had gone to bed. And if I decided to have a sleepover, they had to be up and out before my girls woke up. By this time, sex was all I had to offer and all I was willing to give. There was a small part of me that still wished for the love, joy and comfort of having my own special someone. Being in love was a wonderful feeling. Nevertheless, I had closed the door on the possibility of love. There was an electric fence with a guard dog and keep out signs around my heart. No one was getting in, so a relationship wasn't even on the table for me. Guys had a hard time believing that there was a woman who didn't want to be in a committed relationship. But I had tried it, failed, and I was still suffering through the aftermath. There was no way I was getting tangled up in that again. I guess you would say I had become jaded and quite bitter.

Things started to shift again when my mother got married. Maybe four or five days after her wedding, I got divorced. Yep! I was so happy that my mother finally had someone who loved her so unconditionally. She deserved to have her happily ever after. I can't ever remember seeing her so happy. But in the midst of her happiness, my heart was breaking. While she was away on her honeymoon celebrating the beginning of her new marriage; I was back home at home ending mine. There was this unexplainable ache in my soul as I was sitting in the court room watching New York. Here was this man who I just knew I would spend the rest of my life with, and now we were saying goodbye. It was hard to sit there and not fall apart. It was even worse knowing that he had someone waiting for him and I had no one. But you want to know the worst part? New York had a secret that I didn't find out about until much later. He was already engaged to be married! We hadn't even finalized our divorce and he was planning a wedding! Let me tell you when I did find out, I completely lost it!

First, he didn't include the girls in the wedding. However, he arranged for them to be there. Secondly, he gave instructions for no one to tell me. I remember this rage I felt when I found out. It was like burning, hot bubbling, lava boiling on the inside of me. It kept rising higher and I didn't even try to push it down anymore. It was like everything I was holding in all came rushing to the surface; I couldn't eat or sleep. I was consumed with rage. The closer it got to their wedding the worse it got. All I saw was red; it was during that rage that I decided they both had to die. Yes, I'm so serious! I wanted them dead and I wanted to kill them myself. I had never hated someone as much as I hated New York. He had completely disrespected me and what we shared. And he was so devious with it all. He handled it all wrong.

He had no regard for my feelings. There was no way I was letting him get away with that. See in my mind, his engagement to another woman while we were still married was evidence that he was cheating on me while we were married. Now I know what you're thinking, I cheated on him too, right? Ok, you are correct; however, the two offenses were not the same. In my case, I didn't have sex with anyone else until after we were separated, but he did. See the difference?

Anyway, back to the murder. I planned to kill New York and his new bride on their wedding day. I was going to wear all black and sit at the back of the church. Right before the minister pronounced them husband and wife, I was going to walk up front and shoot them both in the face, first her then him. It had to be in that order because I wanted him to see her die. Then maybe he would feel the pain I felt. Then I was going to kiss my babies and wait for the police to come and get me. Dramatic huh? I know but that's how it played out in my head. And no, I didn't think about what it would do my girls. I didn't think about how my life would be over. All I knew is that the person I hated most in the world would be dead and that's all I wanted. Nevertheless, there were a couple of glitches in my plan. One being I didn't have a gun, and two, I couldn't drive to the church. When I think about it now, its sort of funny. Could I have killed them? Could I have pointed a gun and shot someone's face off? In that heart-wrenching pain, maybe I could have. Lucky for them, I couldn't drive!

I bet you're wondering where was God in all this. Well I have no idea. I'm sure He was right where I left him, but I wasn't looking for Him during this time at all. I didn't want to sing anymore. I didn't want to go to church, read the Bible, or pray. I was tired of trying to be a good person. I didn't want to forgive New York for what he'd done to me, especially for what he wasn't doing for our children. He had left me to deal with all the hard stuff. I was the one raising our kids with no job, living on Section Eight and using food stamps. He didn't give anything extra than the little child support that didn't barely pay rent. He wasn't there for the doctor's appointments, school activities, basketball games, scrapes and bruises, or our broken-hearted daughters. All of that fell on me. I was under the impression that he would at least be a great father to them whether we were together or not. I didn't know how to do this on my own and I didn't want to. But as far as I was concern he was a crappy father and that's what hurt the most. I was in so much pain that I literally, physically ached. I cried all the time, I just couldn't function properly. I was so broken, all I wanted to do is crawl inside of myself and die.

My mother saw what all this was doing to me and she was so worried about me. I wasn't eating much and I barely slept. I wasn't doing well in school. Honestly, I wasn't doing a good job of taking care of my babies either. I just didn't have anything left to give to them. Our divorce, his marriage, raising the girl, it was all too much! My mother was concerned for the mental and emotional well- being of my children. They didn't understand why mommy was so sad and it couldn't have been good for them seeing me like this. I tried my best to protect them from what I was feeling, but soon I just couldn't hide it anymore. I was a wreck! My mother came to take the girls for a while. It was during this time that I completely fall apart. I shut myself away in the apartment, locked the door, closed the blinds and let it all go. I threw things, screamed at the ceiling, and finally broke into a weeping mess. I cried for days, so much that the tears just stopped coming. Then, I just laid in bed and moaned because it hurt that badly. I blamed God. I blamed myself, but mostly I blamed New York. I hated him with a deep-rooted passionate, hatred. I can't explain the depth and intensity of this pain or why it hurt so badly. It just did! My emotions were flying all over the place, from one extreme to another. Rage, sadness, guilt and bitterness were all running through me like a flood. I felt rejected and unworthy. I felt useless and abandoned. I didn't want to talk to anyone or see anyone. I sat alone in the darkness with my pain. It was like being trapped at the bottom of an empty well, closed in, darkness all around and the light was an unreachable flicker in the distance.

It's funny how the mind messes with you when you're in a dark place. All sorts of crazy thoughts race through your head. For me, I wondered why God allowed me to be born in the first place? What was the purpose of all this stuff I went through whether I contributed to it or not? How much was I supposed to endure? Then, I thought about death and how easy it would be to just slip away and why shouldn't I? Maybe if I took more Benadryl this time I would die. It was already the only way I was getting any sleep anyway. So, why not just take a lot extra? Or maybe I should just blow my brains out, but the thought of that not turning out right scared the crap out of me. The voices in my head were screaming me at me to just do it. I didn't though, but I sure wanted too. I also thought about my father during this time. Same thought, if he didn't want me why would any other man? I thought I just wasn't lovable, or maybe I didn't deserve love. Maybe I was not enough or smart enough. Maybe all my health issues made me impossible to love. Why didn't he stay? Why didn't my father want me? It had to be a reason that my father didn't love me and whatever his reason, it was the same reason New York didn't love me anymore either. I needed answers. I needed someone to explain to me why I was right here at this place in my life. And for some crazy reason, I thought my father had all the answers. But if he did, he never gave them to me.

By this time, I knew him a little, well as much as you can know someone who wouldn't talk to you much. He had made it clear that he wasn't offering any explanation of what happened or why he wasn't a part of my life. His exact words were, "That's the past, so leave it there." Me being me, I didn't press the issue although I felt that I was entitled to have my questions answered. I did my best to take what I was given and to let the rest go. It wasn't an easy thing to do, but I tried. My brother made it easier for me. I had already met him some time back and that was an interesting story, but one I'm not at liberty to share. The important part is that someone thought it was time we met, so I was introduced to one who introduced me to another one. There were still two siblings for whatever reason who didn't have much to do with me. It hurt, but I guess I couldn't blame them. I was a stranger claiming to be their sister with no proof. I was happy to have two of the four who wanted to be a part of my life. I was grateful for the opportunity to establish a relationship with them. It was through this relationship that I got pieces of my father. My father stopped by the apartment a couple of times. I can't ever remember him coming inside though; I went downstairs to see him. One of those times he came by with boxes of shoes in his trunk. I'm not sure why. I can't remember if I bought a pair or he gave them to me, but those shoes are alone and the only thing I have from him. I don't wear them because they are my most prized possessions.

Even the relationship with my brothers or the pieces of my father weren't enough to fill the empty place in my heart. I thought the connection with the other side of my family would somehow heal the broken place, but it didn't. If anything, having them in my life made things harder for me. Now, I felt I had to audition for them, you know to see what parts of me they liked and what parts they didn't. I didn't care much about impressing my father, since he was barely putting forth any effort. It was different when it came to my brothers; they were all I had so it was important to me to be a good sister. I loved them so much and I held on tightly to them. I know it had to be weird for them having me telling them how much I loved them all the time. But that's what I did, because that's all I knew. I told them every chance I had. I would do absolutely anything for them. Truth is, I just wanted them to love me back. I needed to have their love because I felt their love in some ways compensated for not having the love of my father. Yet, there was still this emptiness.

I started trying to hang out more. I had made some new friends when I moved so I tried some new things. I went to the club a couple of times but I didn't like that. It was too smoky and way too dark for me. I smoked a little weed a couple of times and just didn't see the point of that. I started drinking a little and I liked that a lot. However, my brother didn't allow me to have any of the hard stuff. I could only have wine coolers, so that's what I drank, a lot!! When I was drinking, I wasn't thinking. And when I wasn't thinking I said exactly what I was feeling. This alcoholic boldness was quite liberating. I drank and then called people and told them what I *really* thought of them. Maybe this wasn't the best way to release things but it sure felt good. I was tired of doing what was best for everyone else. It had become exhausting trying to be the better person and do the right thing *all* the time. I had reached my limit with all that and

I was done! It was time for me to be selfish and everyone else be damned. That's how I felt and that's exactly what I did.

I kept certain parts of my life safeguarded. I didn't want anyone to know what I was doing because I didn't want to have to explain my actions to anyone. I didn't want to hear any judgements or convictions from anyone. I knew I was being careless and irresponsible, but I didn't care. I knew I was living a sinful life and I didn't care about that either. I wasn't going to church a lot anyway. I already knew God was disappointed in me and how I was handling things. I didn't have much to say to Him and I didn't see any point in pretending. Yes, I still loved Him but I just didn't have any interest in being good. I just wanted to do what I wanted to do without thinking about consequences. I just wanted to live in the moments that I created. This was especially true when it came to guys. I wanted to be in full control of who I allowed to get close to me and how long they occupied a given space in my life. I liked it that way and no, I had no regard for anyone's feeling besides my own. Anytime I felt like some guy was trying to get closer than I wanted, I cut them off cold.

For instance, I had certain "guy friends" that I allowed in my life based on whatever criteria I had at the time. Some I met online, others I met out somewhere. We talked for a little bit to see if I felt a connection of any kind, and if so, then I decided what I wanted to happen next. Sometimes we got to know each other and remained just friends with no strings attached. Other times we talked and found a connection or an attraction that led to sex. I was careful in my selection process and it took quite some time for things to become physical, but once we did, he was the only guy I was having sex with. Nine times out of ten the sex was unprotected, yea, stupid I know. But since my tubes were tied I wasn't concerned about getting pregnant which scared me more than any STD. I should have been more cautious, but I wasn't. And I have no reason why. Anyway, I would have sex with a guy until one of us didn't want to do it anymore. Usually he wanted to turn our great sex into a relationship, and I wasn't going for that. So, in that case, he had to go. Sometimes things just fizzled out. Other times, I cut it off because I was afraid of getting attached. Great sex can very easily make you think you have feelings when you can't stand the guy.

I had tried a few times, a couple of one-night stands and a couple who I kept around for a while. Jesse was one of those that made the cut. He was a handsome little devil and yes, I do mean literally the devil. He was no one that I would have chosen for myself. But that intoxicating smile just pulled me into him. He was charming and he knew how to make me laugh. He was a pretty sweet guy for the most part. There were just parts of him that made him devilish. He was a smoker, which I hated. He also was affiliated with some sort of gang like organization. He had broken a few laws, not sure which ones because I didn't ask. But the worse part was his drinking. Although he denied it, he was most definitely an alcoholic. He was a nasty drunk and the first guy I had ever dealt with that gave me "Teddy" flashbacks. You would have thought with all these flashing lights I would have turned and run the other way. Nope, I kept full speed ahead!

    He did have a job sometimes but never offered any money for all the time he spent at my apartment. He just wasn't a good guy for me but oh the sex!! The sex turned him into prince charming. I was so hooked on this dude I had lost all my common sense. I'm talking about giving him money, letting him take my cell phone, cooking dinners, washing clothes.... the whole nine. I excused everything he did wrong. I told myself that he was fixable, all I had to do was hang in there with him. I was completely gone over this guy. Man, I am telling you great sex with the wrong guy will mess you up. I'm a living witness. I tried my best to let him go, but I couldn't do it. I didn't care when he lost my brand-new cell phone. I didn't care when he vomited all over my bathroom. I didn't care when he popped up unexpected all times of the night. All I wanted was to have sex just one more time and then I would let him go. That one more time turned into many one more times. He was like a drug, and I was an addict. I had broken all the rules I set for myself. I had convinced myself I was in love with this man. Really, I did!! The funny part is he had the same rules as I did, no feelings just sex. Neither one of us had planned for this and we had no idea what to do. I knew I didn't love him but I think he ended up feeling more for me than he anticipated. So, he left. Just like that he up and moved out of the state. I was devastated over losing him, well at least *one* part of him.

It was around this time that I decided that maybe the way I was doing things might not be the best way. Being with different guys, even just for the companionship wasn't helping what was happening on the inside. As a matter of fact, I'm sure it was only making my heart condition worse, emotionally that is. I knew I needed to get it together, not just for me but for my girls. I had managed to protect them from a lot of things but not *everything*. They knew mommy had friends that stopped by sometimes, but they didn't know some came back late at night while they slept. They also knew that sometimes I got sad and cried a lot. Sometimes the sadness turned to anger and they were the closest targets. I know there were times that I yelled too much, or punished them too harshly. Yes, I spanked my children but I never beat them. And believe me, there is a difference. In any case, I never wanted to hurt them or let them see me hurt but I'm sure they experienced both. I didn't feel I was being a very good mother and I wanted to be better for them.

Of course, my first thought was to go back to church. I missed it and the love I received from all the people there. It was a place I felt most at home, and a time when things didn't hurt quite as bad. I especially missed singing. It always made me feel better, if only for a little while. I went a few times and it felt good to be there, but I didn't feel connected. It felt different, as if something had changed. I don't know how to explain it. Maybe the biggest part of it was the tremendous guilt I still carried for all the mistakes I had made. Or maybe it was because I felt silently judged for those mistakes. I guess it was a combination of many things. I just know I didn't feel like I *wanted* to be there as I felt like I was *supposed* to be there. If I was going to get back into church I was going to go all in and do it the right way. I was going to make things right with God, renew my relationship with Him, and live a Christian life as best as I could. So, I started praying more and reading my Bible more. But the truth was, as hard as I tried, I just wasn't quite there yet and I wasn't going to pretend that I was.

    Remember I mentioned a few one night stands earlier? Well there was this one guy that wasn't going away that easily. We didn't talk everyday but he kept in contact with me every now and again. Let's call him Kurt. He was a very nice guy, and he seemed to always make time for me. He had a good job, came from a good family, and he didn't come with any drama. He was the kind of guy that a woman would be lucky to have, and I knew that so I didn't want to waste his time. I knew I wasn't ready to be that woman. See, he was one of those who wanted a relationship at a time when I wasn't looking for one. But I guess he decided to keep in touch just in case I ever changed my mind. However, I had no intentions on doing that but I must admit I admired his persistence and willingness to wait for me. I thought about it for a minute, but I just didn't think it was possible to build a relationship on such a messy foundation. Let me tell you how it all started.

Kurt

I met Kurt online some time before I moved to Greenwood. We talked on the phone almost every day. He called in the mornings before he went to work, on his lunch break, when he got off work, and before he went to sleep. And whenever I called he usually always answered and if he didn't he always called back just as soon as he could. We stayed on the phone for hours having the best conversations. I could tell him anything, even about other guys. It was great! He told me how pretty I was, how smart I was, and what a good mother I was, and this was all before we even met each other! He thought I was the best thing since slice bread. He was great himself. It was all very good for my self-esteem. He had this way of making me feel so special at a time when I didn't feel like I was worth anything. I truly enjoyed the attention. But for some reason I thought he was just too good to be true. I think that was mainly in part due to the fear I felt when we met, that he would no longer think so highly of me. So, I held off on meeting him for a while. I just wanted to hang on to those good feelings I had before his reality of me changed everything.

After a good long while, I decided I couldn't put it off any longer, he wanted to see me, so I made plans to meet him. I told my mother I needed a break and that I was getting a hotel room for the weekend. She had no idea what I had planned; it wasn't anything she needed to know. As a matter of fact, I didn't tell anyone what I had planned. There was only one person who knew where I was but even she didn't know what I had planned. I told Kurt where I was going to be and had him meet me there at a certain time. Yes, this is where I was completely and utterly insane. I could have been waiting alone for a serial killer, and no one would have known who I was with. But nope, stupid me was still naive and irresponsible. I didn't think about what could have happened. Anyway, it gets worse. No sooner than I opened the door for him, we went at it. I didn't even get a good look at him before we were ripping each other's clothes off. It was crazy! Yes, we had instant, unprotected sex the very first time we met! I don't know. I think I had become so comfortable with him talking over the phone, he didn't feel like a stranger to me. I didn't feel threatened or concerned, I felt safe with him and so that's what happened. We spent the whole weekend together talking, having sex, and sneaking in and out of public places. No one saw us together the entire weekend and that's just how I wanted it. See? Messy foundation!

    After our initial meeting, he would come to see me every now and then. I had to be careful because I still lived at home with my mother and the girls. So, he mostly visited at night after my mother had left for work and the girls were asleep. He drove over two hours just to see me for maybe an hour or so. And yes, there was sex involved! There was only one other person who met him and knew what was going on between us. I kept it quiet because I didn't want to answer any questions about him, and with my family there were bound to be questions. I wasn't ready to settle down or get into anything serious and he was fine with that. He was aware that I talked to other guys and maybe sometimes went out with them, if I chose to. He was also free to do as he pleased. I enjoyed getting know him. He was the kind of guy that I dated if I was interested in dating. Anyway, he was just another guy that occupied a space in my life, he just stuck around way longer than I thought he would.

    Flash forward a year or so later and Kurt was still there. He didn't pressure me or anything, he just waited in the wings hoping maybe one day I would give him a chance. So, I did. I saw Kurt as my opportunity for a fresh start. I had tried to numb the pain with a string of "sexlationships" that did nothing but make things worse. I wanted to be in a committed relationship, to have someone to love and who loved me in return. But I was just so afraid to do that again. Kurt presented me with a chance to try and the promise that he wouldn't hurt me. Now I know no one can promise you that because people unemotionally hurt one another all the time. For some reason I believed him. He was an amazing guy! He had this way of making me feel I was the most beautiful woman in the world. He showered me with compliments all the time. Even when I knew I looked a mess, he found the beauty anyway. He didn't care one bit about my visual impairment. He was like a second set of eyes for me. I never had to remind him of my limitations, he just knew.

Kurt had this way about him, a gentlemanly way that made me feel like a real lady. He was the open your door, pull your chair out kind of guy. He was the whatever you need I will take care of it kind of guy. He catered to me and I wasn't at all used to that. This guy would drive to my apartment just to help me do my homework. Truth is I probably wouldn't have graduated without him. He was always there for me. And did I mention the gifts? He was constantly bringing gifts for me and my friends, leaving money hidden for me all over the apartment. He was a great provider; I longed for nothing. The best part of all, he was amazing with my girls. He accepted them as an extension of me and he treated them extremely well. He brought them gifts as well and he always made sure they had whatever they needed and most of what they wanted. He spoiled them. All in all, he was close to the perfect guy, so much so that I didn't think I deserved him. I couldn't figure out why he was so nice to me or why he went out of his way to do so much for me. I honestly didn't get it! He was everything I wanted in a guy, but nothing I thought I was worthy to have. As you may be able to tell, I was still mentally screwed up from all the baggage I carried.

Kurt didn't care about my baggage; he took it all and did his best to help me carry it. He loved me and he went out of his way to let me know. I remember one time he arranged for me to audition for this major talent show at the Township in Columbia, SC. It was a big deal for me since I had never done anything like it before. I was so nervous the whole ride there, but he wasn't worried at all. He kept telling me how talented I was and that he was sure they were going to choose me for the show. He was right and they did select me. He was more excited than I was. He went out and bought me a new outfit to wear for the showcase. He ensured my family got tickets to be there to see me perform. The whole experience was so great and although I didn't win, I was grateful for the opportunity. But the best part of the whole experience is how he took care of me. See, the auditorium was huge and the lights were turned down very low. I couldn't see well and I was concerned about how I navigate around alone. Well, Kurt made sure that didn't happen. He was right there to escort me to the waiting area. He couldn't stay backstage with me, but he made sure someone else would take care of me. When I finished singing and walked off the stage, he was right there waiting. I don't even know how he found his way to where I was going to be but he did. I was so relieved to see him and that was the moment I knew that I was completely safe with him.

  We dated for a while and things were going well. I grew to care for him a lot. I worked hard to put my past behind me and to let go of all the hurt. I tried my best to be happy with him and not concentrate on those nagging thoughts in my head that were telling me I wasn't good enough. I fought hard not to believe them, but I did. I didn't think I was good enough and that this wasn't going to last. It was a struggle for me and he was constantly reassuring me, but it didn't help. I didn't think I was pretty. I hated my eyes, even more so because one of them didn't work. I didn't have curves or a desirable body. I didn't have a job or anything to bring to the table. I didn't understand why he wanted me when I didn't even like me. But even so, he hung in there with me. I sure don't know why because I was driving myself crazy, so I knew he had to be frustrated with me. Well if he was, he hid it well because all he showed me was love and support. Who wouldn't want a guy like that? It wasn't too long before we started making plans for our future. I couldn't believe all this was happening, but he solidified it when he proposed!

    Right in the middle of the Lion King he dropped down on one knee and asked me to marry him. The girls were standing there with huge grins on their faces waiting for me to answer. They looked so happy and it made me happy to see that they were happy. I found out later Kurt had spoken to them before he proposed to make sure it was okay with them. I thought that was the sweetest thing ever. Well, of course I said yes! The first call I made was to my mother who was extremely happy for me. My entire family as well as my friends were all happy for me. The thought of being married again made me all giddy inside. Now my girls would have the family they deserved with a step-father who adored them. I wanted this more for them than I did for myself. I was ready this time. I was going to take my time and do it right. I was going to enjoy the engagement, take things slowly as we planned the wedding. I was in no hurry; I wanted to be sure that this was it. I was so excited and he was happy that I had agreed to be his wife. For the first time in a very long time, I had hope that I could have the happiness I have always wanted.

Kurt and I decided to do this right, we had to get back in right relationship with God. So, we starting attending church together regularly. It felt good to be back in church and even better having Kurt there beside me. Having God in the middle of us seemed to make things better, and they were already good. I was genuinely happy and it didn't take as much work as it used to. Things were good! We even decided to take a vow of celibacy until our wedding day. Now that was a sacrifice! I mean I had become accustomed to our regular rendezvous when he came to visit. Although I knew it was the right thing to do, I wasn't thrilled about doing it. There were a few slip ups when we first started but eventually we got a handle on it. Truth be told, it was a good feeling knowing that we were trying to live a Christian lifestyle together. It was also comforting to know that God was pleased that we were trying. By this time, I was tired of the way I had been doing things. I wasn't proud of a lot of the choices I had made. Now, I had a second chance to get it together and I was ready.

Unfortunately, Kurt and I never made it to the

altar. A series of events led me to believe that marriage wasn't the right move for us. I want to make it clear that we could have worked things out and gotten married eventually. However, I am the reason that never happened. I loved Kurt, I did but nowhere near as much as he loved me. He absolutely adored me and I was extremely grateful for his love, but something was missing for me. I'm not sure how to explain other than to say that it seemed that my feelings hit a wall. It's like my heart wouldn't allow me to love him past a certain point. I wasn't sure why. So, when certain situations occurred, they justified what I was feeling. For example, there was this one time we were on a weekend getaway and we got into this huge argument. We were laying opposite each other (feet to head) across the bed after working out at the hotel gym. I made the comment that his feet smelled. He got very upset and began yelling and cursing at me. I was confused on what I said wrong to cause such a drastic reaction. There was another time when I accidently said, "Yes ma'am" when addressing him. He went off! Do I look like a woman to you?" "Why would you say that to me?" "Do I act like a woman, huh? Say? Say?" We were in the middle of the mall while he was screaming at me. I was so shocked I didn't know what to do.

    He had these outbursts every now and then. He got so angry over something I considered small. It was like a child having a tantrum. He may throw the keys across the room, raise his voice or hang up on me if we were on the phone. Sometimes he would just get in his truck and leave without saying a word. I never knew how he would react in any given situation. But when he was mad, that's when I felt he spoke his truth. I remember this one time we were arguing about something he said, "You should be glad I wanna be with you. I can be with any of these girls out here. It's not like you're a dime or something." This meant, "You're not the prettiest girl but I'm with you anyway." That statement alone totally negated every wonderful thing he had ever said to me. Of course, he apologized saying he didn't mean it and begged for forgiveness. And of course, I didn't believe him. See I believe he meant every word, he just got angry enough to say it out loud. I didn't trust him anymore. If he could lie to me about his true feelings, what else was he lying about. Not to mention there was already this woman lurking around that he had a questionable relationship with. All these things combined coupled with the looming doubt about him in my heart, I thought it best to just let it all go. Was he a good guy? Yes, he was! Could we have worked it all out? Sure, we could have! But with my track record, I wasn't taking any chances.

Chapter Thirteen
Love Is…

Imagine pulling up to your apartment to find a crowd of people waiting for you outside. Everyone's eyes are on you when you step out of the car. The crowd parts so you can come though, all eyes still on you. As you approach the stairs leading to your apartment, you note flickers of candlelight leading upstairs to your apartment. Candles and rose petals align the pathway to your door. When you enter your apartment, you see candles all over the place, dining room, hallway, and a heart made of candles in the middle of your living room floor. You stand in complete awe of the romantic setting that you see before you. You're escorted to the table for dinner. You can barely enjoy your dinner because you are mesmerized by the gorgeous man sitting across from you. His smile pulls you into him and yourself lost in his eyes. Before you realize what is happening you find yourself in your bedroom. The room has been transformed to match the rest of the apartment. Rose petals are carefully spread across the bed, candles are burning all over the room, little crystal bowls are filled with your favorite fruit, and romantic music is playing softly. It's the perfect romantic scene right out of a movie. Your heart is beating so fast you can hardly catch your breath. He walks over to you, takes you in his arms and kisses you passionately. Your mind is racing a mile a minute, no one has ever done anything like this for you before. Just when you thought you would never fall in love again…

Seven came along at an unexpected time in my life. I had just broken off my engagement and wasn't looking for anyone at all. I had refocused my energies on finishing up my associates degree and devoting more time to my children. They were growing up so fast and I felt like I had to soak in every moment. Not to mention that I felt like I needed to stop focusing on myself and all I had going on and just make it all about them. They had gone through a lot of changes over the past few years. As much as I tried to shield them, I could see how these changes were impacting them. Don't get me wrong, they were happy little women, but they each had their own way of dealing with things.

Alexis, although the oldest was my little, big baby. She required much more of my time and attention. She still struggled with her father's absence and his remarrying. There were times when she still cried for him but not as much as when he first left. And now there was a step-mother for her to get used to. Sometimes, she acted out on her visits with her father. And then she was extra clingy when she was with me. I didn't mind the extra hugs and kisses if they made her feel better. Other times, I would roll over in bed to find her snuggled up next to me. I guess she just needed to be close, and I didn't mind that either. I would do anything to make her feel safe and loved because I was all too familiar with the "I want my daddy" feeling.

Alexis was also struggling in school; she had a hard time keeping up with the other children. Although she had learned braille, reading was still very difficult for her. Math also presented its own challenges, though she loved it. She had trouble grasping some of the concepts. Helping her with homework had become a group effort in the apartment complex. My friends often stepped in to help me with her. It took hours for her to finish because she couldn't see certain things and she didn't always comprehend things she was unable to see for herself. It was complicated and frustrating, but mostly painful to watch her struggle when she was trying so hard. Greenwood definitely presented better educational opportunities for her, but it still wasn't enough. I knew I had to do more to help my daughter and it was going to come at a major sacrifice to me.

We had taken a tour of the South Carolina School for the Deaf and Blind, which seemed to be a great place to meet her educational needs. This opportunity would also give her a chance to meet other children like her. While there were good opportunities, there was one huge drawback. I had to allow her to live an hour and a half away from me during the week. She would only be with me on the weekends and during school breaks. I wasn't crazy about trusting strangers to take care of my baby. And I wasn't sure how she would adapt to yet another major change in her life. Also, I didn't want her to think that I was sending her away. I was torn for quite some time. I prayed long and hard and finally reached a peace about it. Still, it was one of the hardest decisions that I had ever had to make. I had to do what was best for her, and I truly believed sending her there was for her optimum benefit. Alexis, at age nine, was a lot stronger and braver than I gave her credit...she adapted to the change and accepted the challenge.

Then there was little Ms. Alysha. She was such a serious, little lady, not too childlike at all. She rarely went outside to play with the other children, and if she ended up outside she only sat on the steps and watched the others play. She didn't like to get dirty. She didn't like to sweat. Actually, the only reason she ended up outside was if I made her go or if she felt she needed to keep an eye on her sister. Her preference was to be inside watching television or reading a book. She was an excellent student and enjoyed school very much. There were even times she helped her sister with homework. As a matter of fact, she was her sister's keeper. She was always concerned about her and very overly protective of her. Alexis was the only close friend that Alysha had. I began to notice very early on how guarded she was. There were only a select few that she allowed to get close to her. As far as I could tell, she was a happy child, just a very observant one.

If Alysha was harboring any feelings about her father, she didn't show them much. Of course, there were moments when she cried for him, but those moments were rare. She seemed to be one of those "take things as they are" kind of people. She didn't talk about her father much or ask any questions. She never complained about her new step-mother, and she seemed to enjoy her visits with them. I waited for some sort of sign to let me know how she was processing things, but there wasn't any. Well except for the obvious one, she was extremely protective when it came to her sister and me. She preferred being wherever I was. She wasn't one of those little girls who went to sleepovers with friends. I could barely convince her to spend the night with her Nana. And when she did go for a sleepover, she was certain to make sure that I was going to be okay without her. She was more concerned about me being alone than going and having fun. She felt I needed her and that I would miss her too much while she was gone. It was sweet the way she loved me. I just wanted her to be a normal, happy, carefree child. But instead she was more like a responsible adult with childlike moments trapped inside a little girl's body.

Alysha just went with the flow. So, when I told her we were leaving Greenwood and going back to McCormick, she didn't protest at all. She wasn't as agreeable when I told her Alexis would be going away for a while. She didn't like that her sister wasn't going to be close. She was even more concerned about who would be watching out for her. Although she was the youngest, watching out for sister had always been her job. She didn't trust anyone else to do that. I had always tried to instill in them the importance of taking care of one another and looking out for each other. I taught them to love each other and to never let anyone come between them. They were as different as night and day, but the one thing that bonded them was their devotion to one another. So, I understood her concern and assured her that the separation wouldn't be for long. My girls were my entire world and my love for them surpassed any void I may have felt. I knew it was time for me to make some serious changes.

In the midst of these changes came Seven. It all started off innocently. I needed to pick up another class, so I chose one that my very good friend was taking. She made the class sound interesting, so I gave it a try. I didn't notice him at first, but that goes without saying considering my vision had changed so much. I couldn't see as well out of my left eye as I had when I first lost my vision in the right eye. It had been eight years since I had become legally blind. I'm sure all the reading I had for school had contributed to this recent decrease in vision, but it didn't matter because I was determined to finish my degree. Anyway, my friend and I soon became friendly with Seven and his friend. We grabbed breakfast together or just hung out between classes. The socializing was nice and there was no pressure for anything extra. Seven and I were also both taking Probability and Statistics, which I was struggling with terribly. He was doing a little better than I was, but we both still needed some help. I had a classmate who was doing much better than the both of us and she started tutoring me. So, whenever I finished my work, I let him know. He then stopped by my apartment to copy it. That's how it all started, him coming by that is. Soon he was giving me rides home from school and hanging out for a while, which I didn't have a problem with. He was fun to hang out with, but he was way too young for me to even consider dating, that's if I even wanted to date. At the moment, I had no interest.

Needless to say, Seven was a nice guy. He was easy on the eyes too, tall, dark, and handsome. Cliché but true. He was lean, just enough muscular build to know he worked out some. His stomach was as flat as a board; I could tell even with his shirt on. I didn't know exactly how old he was but I could tell he was younger by the way he dressed. He wore baggy jeans, loose shirts, and sneakers most of the time. He had an amazing smile, the kind that made you smile whether you wanted to or not. Oh yes, he was a pleasure to look at it. That's as far as it went for me. Besides, even if I wanted to date, (which I want to strongly emphasize that I did not), I didn't think I was the type of girl he would go for. I just didn't look the part, which is why it totally threw me off guard when he kissed me one day. Yea, it was totally unexpected. Okay, maybe not TOTALLY! See, we had become friends, we talked on the phone, and maybe even flirted a little. Nothing major. And one day, I mentioned how I couldn't dance and he decided to teach me. Well, just know that slow dancing can possibly lead to French kissing. I'm just saying!

In any case, it was of no concern to me. It was a

kiss, nothing more than that. I wasn't going to make more out of it than it was. And if this young guy thought he was going to pull me in with a kiss, he had another thing coming. I had grown woman stuff to handle. I had to focus on my girls, myself, and finishing school. These were my main priorities. I didn't have time nor did I plan to make time to play out his "older woman" fantasies. I wanted to keep working on my relationship with God, going to church, reading my Bible, praying and all the other stuff good Christians do. That's what I wanted now, to be a good Christian, so maybe just maybe I could get my life back together. And getting tangled up in mind blowing sex with a young, sexy, chocolate man-god was not being a good Christian. And how did I know the sex would be mind-blowing? Trust me, I had a pretty good idea it would be. Nope, it was not going to happen!

I also had a plan; I was moving back to McCormick to save up money so Alysha and I could move to Spartanburg to be with Alexis. I was putting all my past mess behind me, especially all the self-inflicted heartache, unnecessary drama, and careless irresponsible self-destructive man choices. Yep, I had to get it together, starting over, and for me that included absolutely no men!

But that smile though, the way he smiled at me just sucked me in. He made me laugh because he wasn't afraid to be silly. We sat on the phone for hours talking about all sorts of things, some serious and some with no meaning at all. We'd become good friends. I could talk to him about anything and he just got it, no explanation necessary. It was like there were no years between us. He was amazing with my girls as well. He came and picked them up for school in the morning so that wouldn't have to wait on the bus. He brought them candy or little toys. He sat and talked to them, having real conversation with them on their level. I loved watching them together. They seemed to genuinely like him. That wasn't hard to believe because he was a great guy.

The most wonderful thing about him is that he was a Christian. He wasn't perfect by a long shot, but he was trying his best to be better. I didn't have to make him understand where I was trying to get to with God because he was trying, too. I didn't have to explain to him why there were certain things I didn't do or was trying not to do because he was trying, too. I didn't have to convince him to go to church because he already attended regularly. As a matter of fact, he had a very active role at his church which I found quite impressive. He seemed to be just the right kind of guy for me and it would have been perfect if I were ready. My heart was still shut down for repair and I couldn't rush the process. I just wasn't ready and I knew that for sure. All I could think was no, no, noooooo!

Okay so remember the imaginary scene at the beginning of this chapter? Yea that one, well it happened and that's how he won me over. Of course, I couldn't let him know that. I fought hard to keep myself from showing the slightest reaction to the scene before me. I didn't do a very good job, though. I tried to make it seem like it was no big deal, but the truth was no one had ever done anything like that for me before. It was a very big deal! The way he had taken the time to plan it and put so much effort into making it all so breathtakingly romantic, just made my heart flutter. It was beautiful and I absolutely loved it, and he saw that all over my face. So, of course, we had sex that night. It was inevitable and there was no way around it. Well there probably was, but who am I kidding? I knew we were having sex the moment I walked in the apartment that evening. But why? I had to or at least thought I ought to. How could I not after he had presented me with such a romantic gesture of whatever he was trying to accomplish. I didn't even stop to think that maybe sex was his end goal all along. I honestly didn't care because I wanted to have sex with him and so I did. It wasn't just to reward him for a job well done, but also for absolute pleasure for me. I figured if this guy wanted to go down this road with me, then here we go! I was going to teach him a lesson. I was going to have sex with him, as much as I wanted but I would NEVER be his girlfriend. I was going to use him for my own pleasures and when I was done, I would cut him off like all the others before him. He wasn't going to get my heart, nope!

    I bet you're wondering what happened to all those God changes I was talking about earlier, huh? Well I still wanted to change and I had in a lot of ways, but I didn't quite get all the way there. I was in church and doing all the other Christian stuff. I was in a pretty good place with God, minus the whole sex thing. See sex, especially really, good sex can mess your mind up and throw a monkey wrench into any well-intentioned plan to live the Christian life. And I must admit the devil sure knew how to get me off track and I sure knew how to let him. Every time we had sex was supposed to be the last time until the next time, the cycle began! I told myself that this was going to be a quick fling and he'd eventually lose interest and move on to the next girl. I didn't take into consideration that he may wanted to get into anything serious. I figured he was too young to want to settle down with an older woman, especially one with two young children. So, it all had to be about sex and nothing else, right? Even though I wasn't trying to revisit my past behaviors, I decided Seven would be the last guy I would play this crazy sex game with. I was going to have wonderful mind-blowing sex with him until it was over and then be done with it. Wrong!

Seven had a different plan all together. He continued showing up and not just for sex. He still came to take the girls to school. He came to help with homework or to just hang out. He still called every day, and we still talked for hours. He was consistent and patient. I had explained to him how I wasn't ready for a relationship and how I wanted to get my life back on track, and he respected that. He even understood that although we were having great sex that there would come a time that I would cut that off.

He still came, knowing all I had going on spiritually and emotionally. He continued to show up for me, whenever I needed him. He was there. I had to remind myself that it was too soon to get into something with this guy. I hadn't even completely gotten rid of Kurt, who continued to pop up from time to time. My feelings were completely tangled up in what I should do or not do. We were spending a lot of time together, even more after I moved. I didn't know how to say no I can't do this, this is too much, or just back off until I figured things out. I thought I could handle the friendship, the sex, the post breakup baggage and everything else I had going on. It was his actions that got me. Seven was there through all of it and he became more than just a friend with excellent benefits, he was so much more.

When I say we fell into a relationship, that's exactly what happened. We were spending a lot of time together, practically every day. Seven made it a point to stop by each day before he went to work and if he didn't come see me, I went to see him. He called while driving to work, on his breaks at work and after work while he was driving home. In between calls, there were sweet little text messages letting me know he was thinking of me. It was all quite faltering and I will admit I enjoyed the attention. It still boggled my mind that he wanted me. I just didn't think I was pretty enough for someone like him. And I wasn't trying to invest my heart into something that would eventually come to an end. But as time passed, I found myself turning down advances from other guys, mostly those from the past who wanted to do the sex thing again. I don't know exactly when it happened, but Seven had become the only guy that I was interested in. I will admit I still struggled a lot with the age difference. I was constantly reminding him of how old I was and how my life was way too complicated for someone his age. He just laughed it off and told me how age didn't matter when you are connected to someone. Then one day while we were talking, he said, "You know you're my girlfriend, right?" And I took in a long, deep breath and sighed, "Yea, I know."

Our Love Story

It was something special about this guy that set him apart from any other guy I had ever been involved with. There were a number of things that caught my attention, like his strong self-confidence. He knew he was a good-looking guy and that other girls wanted him. He wasn't overly cocky about it; in fact, he was quite modest. However, he was extremely arrogant when it came to his goals to do something great. He always spoke futuristically about what he was going to become and how successful he would be. I liked that about him; I found it very sexy which only drew me to him more. But his confidence wasn't just in himself, it was also in me. He thought the best of me, always reminding me that I had things to offer the world. He often told me how God had a plan for me and that there was a reason for all the things that I have endured. He used to say that I was a miracle.

It's funny how one person can look at your life and see it so completely different from you when you lived it. And it's something special to have someone believe in you the way Seven believed in me.

The thing that set him apart and allowed me to go on this amazing adventure with him was his heart. He had an incredibly huge, loving heart with a great capacity and willingness to love. He was genuinely a kind and generous person. He was a giver, and not just of gifts but of himself. He made time for us, no matter what else was going on. And when I say us, I mean my children with whom he developed his own separate relationship with. He took the time to get to know them individually, which was new to them since most people tended to lump them both together. For Seven, they were not just the children of his girlfriend, they were separate little people who he thought it important enough to get to know. And he did get to know them and eventually earned their trust. Truly, that was the key element that sealed the deal for me. Any man who could look at my girls and count them as valuable and love them as he did was already a winner in my book.

Seven was reliable and consistent. I could always count on him to do exactly what he said he would. He made it a point of always showing up and being present in my life. He became someone I depended on, someone I trusted and the person who truly earned my heart. He worked for it, because God knows I fought him every step of the way. I just couldn't wrap my mind around the fact that he chose me out of all other desirable options. I didn't understand it, which goes to show you what I thought of myself. My self-esteem was damaged in a way that I didn't even realize. I thought sex was all he wanted and once he got enough, he would be gone. I thought sex was all I had to offer and once I got tired of that I would get tired of him. I had so many negative words running through my head. "You aren't pretty like your mama." "You are lucky to be with me," "You might look a little better with your glasses off" or "Your own father didn't want you." "You'll I never be good enough." These are the words that played over and over every day in my mind. Words from so many people that amounted to me feeling I was never good enough. I struggled to replace the self-destroying thoughts with positive affirmations, but the negative was always louder. Seven saw something different in me. He continued to show up and was constantly trying to dispel the negative thoughts and opinions that I had formed of myself.

This guy was so romantic, an area I had little experience with and hardly any exposure to. I can't count the number of romantic gestures he did to prove to me that he was serious about me. I remember there was this one time he took me to the park. Once we arrived, he had a candle light picnic waiting with music playing in the background. Another time he bought me a purse, filled it with my favorite candy and put a ring at the bottom. He sent flowers and wrote the sweetest poems. One night he showed up with a cheesecake in the trunk of his car with roses and candles everywhere. He was a big romantic and that's how he expressed himself to me. I absolutely loved it; he opened up a whole new world of love to me. It was all so sweet, yet so overwhelming. I had never been exposed to this level of dating and romance. It was a lot to take, in but I enjoyed every single moment of it.

I remember one time when I was sick. I think I had gotten a cold or something; I'm not quite sure. But anyway, I was in a lot of pain and had spent most of the day in bed. Seven came by like he usually did before work and I just felt miserable. He sat on the edge of my bed staring at me. He told me how pretty I was, which I know had to be a lie because I looked a mess. But he insisted that I was beautiful. Then he took my hand and started praying for me. I remember lying there thinking, "Is this dude seriously praying for me right now?' I watched him as he prayed with such intensity and what I thought had to be love. It was something about this guy praying over me that touched me in such a way that I never experienced before. That prayer shifted things for me, took away any doubt and all hesitations that I had. He was it for me and there was no way of stopping what I was feeling. My heart was so full that I did my very best not to cry, but of course I did. When he was done, he looked at me and said, "You're going to be okay baby!" He kissed me on the forehead and left. It was that day, in that very moment, that I fell head over heels completely in love with him.

I was determined not to rush things this time. I

had a bad habit of jumping heart first into relationships without giving them time to grow. This time was going to be different. I was going to go slowly into this relationship and make sure that God was incorporated in it all. However, this was a challenge for both of us. We knew that there was a way of living that was expected of a Christian, but neither of us were there quite yet. Of course, sex was a huge issue, and I don't even know which of us struggled with it more. For a while we didn't put forth the effort to live "right" before God. For us, sex was an expression of our love for one another. It wasn't something we planned as much as we were drawn into. It's like we were magnets being pulled to each other. There was this attraction that went far beyond the physical. It was like our souls were intertwined with one another. I could feel his love for me with every touch, every kiss; it was amazing. And I was like an addict, I needed more and more of him. It was never enough. And it felt wonderful being with him, and having him inside of me made me feel desirable, beautiful, and loved. I had never experienced anything quite so intense before, and I didn't want to give that up, not even for God.

When I tell you, I lost all my good sense when it came to Seven, it was gone. I found myself doing things that I never thought I would. We had what he liked to call "sexual escapades." I can't begin to count how many times we had sex in places that we shouldn't have. We had no regard for where we were or who was around. The trill was in almost getting caught. Outside, in a house full of people, driving in the car, in closets, motel quickies, whenever and wherever we felt the urge, we made it happen. Sometimes he had to talk me into one of his crazy ideas because this was all new to me. Although I had grown to enjoy sex very much, I was sexually shy. He awakened something inside of me that I didn't realize was there. I loved it! We made it interesting with all sorts of games and role playing, it was totally insane! We even went as far as making a sex tape, which is something I never dreamed of doing in a million years. I was completely against it at first, but he wanted to try it. I will admit the idea of it was a turn on, so I was more than willing to participate. I promise I'm not trying to put you all in my business, but I need to stress how this guy had me all wrapped up in love.

Time passed and we spent so much time together. We went out to dinner, the movies, the mall, mostly with the girls but sometimes just the two of us. Sometimes we just rode around and talked. We talked about everything. We didn't make any major decisions without speaking to the other person first. We didn't do anything without sharing it with the other. He made a point of always letting me know where he was, who he was with and what he was doing. And I did the same. He knew my friends and I knew his. There were no secrets between us. He knew about ALL my colorful past. I held nothing back. I never had to wonder about his commitment to me because he reassured me with his actions. I trusted him completely. He was everything I could have ever wanted and never thought existed. I fell more and more in love with him as time passed by. And I knew he loved me too, I just knew it without one single doubt.

Seven and I had created our own little world. Most of the time there was no one in it but our girls, him and me. That's what he called them "our girls." He stepped up with my children in a way I didn't think any man could, more than their father had. If they had something going on at school, he would do his best to be there. If there was some extracurricular activity they had going on, he was there, too. Teacher parent conferences, he was right there. Whenever they needed something, he made sure they had it. School clothes, school supplies, or money for whatever, he made sure they had it. Even when there were things they didn't need, they got those, too. He made Christmas an event for them every year. Homemade gingerbread houses, colorful Christmas trees, scavenger Christmas present hunts, whatever he could do to make it special for them, he did it. They were a priority for him. They grew to love him more and I was so happy to know he loved them, too.

We were a family, not a perfect one, but a family still the same. When I moved to Spartanburg, SC, he made it a point to be there as much as possible. He lived in another city but would come on the weekends to stay with us. Sometimes he popped up in the middle of the week, driving late at night after he got off just because he wanted to see us. We had breakfast together, cooked dinner together, watched movies together, went to church together and we all enjoyed being with each other. The girls loved having him around. He was always doing little things for them, arranging some game or special surprise for them. He was constantly acting silly with them, sometimes it was like having three kids instead of two. There were water gun fights, Uno games, bad singing contests, whatever he came up with to have fun or make them laugh. I loved him for that. On those rare occasion when the girls were gone over night, we stay up late just talking. We talked about our future together, our hopes and dreams and the things we wanted to do together. There wasn't a plan made that didn't include the girls; he was always thinking of them. Once he told me I was his moon, but they were his stars. I was so happy with the family we were creating. All we needed to do now was make it official!

We had been together a couple of years before I started talking marriage. I knew he was the person I wanted to spend the rest of my life with, no question. I was even more sure that I was the person he wanted, too. I took into consideration that he was younger. I needed to give him time. It was hard because all I wanted was to be his wife. I was already doing wifely stuff, washing his clothes, cleaning his apartment when I visited and our finances were tangled up as well. It was like we were married already but we weren't. I just kept telling myself it was just a matter of time and so I waited. Did I wait with a good attitude? Nope, not always. Patience was never my strong suit. I wanted what I wanted. I was tired of the distance. I wanted him there with us every day. Things were shifting in me, call it getting older or whatever. I just wanted to be settled. But more than anything, I was no longer content with how I felt so disconnected from God. I needed to be in a right relationship with God and my relationship with Seven was starting to get in the way of that. Yes, we were both Christians, but we were no longer seeing things eye-to-eye concerning fornication. In the eyes of God, sex outside of marriage is a sin. And I just didn't want to live in sin anymore.

Things started to change about three years in. I was struggling, not only with my position with God but with my position in life. I didn't feel purposeful. I felt stuck not knowing what I was supposed to be doing with my life. I had become so wrapped up with being a mother to my girls and trying to make Seven see me as his wife, that I was lost. As you may recall reading earlier, I said I wasn't ready for a relationship, yet that's exactly what I walked into. Well the truth is I brought a lot of baggage with me that began to weigh on both of us. I wasn't happy and Seven knew it and although I tried to hide it, I couldn't. I became distant. We argued about different things and I just stopped talking to him for extended periods of time. Other times, I tried to break up with him but he wouldn't let me. I became depressed, just sitting around the apartment all day doing nothing. I waited for him to call or for the girls to come home from school. I managed to pull myself together so they wouldn't notice anything. I cried myself to sleep at night and all day long when I was alone, pulled myself together as much as I could, then did it all over again the next day. I wanted to die. I didn't see any reason for being alive. I didn't feel I was contributing to the world in any way. I hated being in Spartanburg. I felt alone in this new city. I missed my friends and family, my church family, and nothing seemed right for me. Seven was right there trying to put me back together, encouraging and helping me, but I couldn't shake the feeling that I would be better off dead.

It was a dark time for me but a familiar place. It was a place that I thought I would never find myself again but a place I felt strangely comfortable in. I stopped trying to pull myself out of it. I had mastered the art of the mask. I learned how and when to cover up what I was feeling and present what the world expected of me. I guess you think I had control over it, but I didn't. The feeling of deep sadness and pain was always with me; I just hid it well. I had started taking Benadryl some time beforehand when I was having trouble sleeping. I found that it had other benefits for me. Not only did Benadryl help me sleep and take care of my allergies, but it also had a way of drying up my emotions. I know it sounds crazy, but it's true. I found that when I was taking the medicine that I didn't cry as much, hardly at all. I didn't feel pain or sadness, as a matter of fact I didn't feel anything at all. So, I took Benadryl every day, morning and night. Sometimes I took it during the day if I felt anxious or upset. Before long, I was taking it all the time and more per dose than directed. After a while I was a walking zombie, but no one noticed and that's all I wanted.

Taking care of my girls was the only job I had and the only thing that kept me from completely losing my mind. Seven didn't want to marry me for his own reasons I guess, but I somehow made it my fault. I felt being a wife was something I was good at and rather enjoyed the first time around. So, I just knew I would be an even better one to this man who I loved so very much. But all he kept telling me was to wait. And I didn't know how long I was supposed to do that or if I could do it. I just knew being his wife would make me happy again, give me purpose and fulfillment. Making another person responsible for my happiness is a tremendous amount of pressure to put on someone, but I wasn't thinking about that at the time. I had convinced myself that being a wife and mother were the only two things I was good at and all I was purposed to do. But Seven didn't agree, he felt there was more I should be doing. Honestly, I didn't want to do anything else, mostly because I didn't think I was capable of anything more. Anyway, why wasn't that enough? Why didn't he understand that I was willing to give him my life, be his help mate, support his dreams, be his cheerleader? What man wouldn't want that? I was prepared to be devoted to him forever. He was all I wanted but as much as he loved me and I knew he did, he didn't want to marry me.

I don't know how to convey what we were for each other. He was my very best friend and we loved each other beyond words. It was a deep abiding love, the kind I knew would stay with me forever. It was the kind of love I had always wanted. It was an all-consuming, unconditional kind of love. I would do absolutely anything for this man and I did. If there was something he needed, I made sure he had it. If there was something he wanted, he got that too. I enjoyed buying him little gifts or doing things for him just to see that beautiful smile. The best part is it went both ways. Even as I was going through this rough time, he never gave up on me. He professed his love and devotion to me repeatedly, and I believed him. There's no greater feeling than knowing someone who loves you so completely. Seven knew all my dirty little secrets, all my hurts and fears, all my baggage and he still chose to love me. But I couldn't deny that things were changing between us. I couldn't make love to him anymore without feeling tremendous guilt and often I cried. Tears after sex didn't make him feel good, but I couldn't help it. I knew this isn't how God had intended it to be. I had done it the wrong way for so long that I had grown tired of telling God I was sorry. I was ready to truly live my life for God, which meant no premarital sex. Yet, that didn't go over very well. He understood it and agreed that I was right but wasn't ready to make the sacrifice. Oddly enough, I understood that, too. Making love had become an expression of our love for each other and I guess he didn't want to give that up and neither did I. But I knew I needed, too. I felt I was going to have to choose between the man I loved and the God who had always loved me.

Things became very tense between us. Reflecting on it all, I know I played a major role in the breakdown of our relationship. I put a lot of pressure on time to save me from myself. Although I never wanted to be the girl who needed a man to save her, that's exactly who I had become. I pushed and pulled at him so much that it had to have taken a toll on him, even though he didn't say so. Sometimes I wanted him close while other times I didn't want him anywhere near me. Something in me was broken and I'm not even sure how or when it happened. Or maybe I was just never whole to start with. I was so hot and cold that I even got on my own nerves. It's like I had no control over it. I was barely getting any sleep, the voices in my head were screaming at me all the time. Still I was trying to hold it together. And even though I knew he still loved me, I could feel him slipping away. We weren't connecting like we used to and I was convinced that he was being unfaithful to me. Of course, I confronted him with my suspicions to which he insisted I was paranoid. And for a while I thought he was right. My mind was playing tricks on me. The more I confronted him, the more he denied. I even made a surprise visit to his apartment.

I got a ride down to where he lived. I let myself in with the key he had given me and waited for him to get there. While I waited, I went through everything.

I noticed he had taken down my pictures, put away my things in the back of his closet, and found condoms in the bathroom (we didn't use condoms). There was not one trace of my existence in the entire apartment. I was furious. First, I thought about burning the apartment down. Then I decided stabbing him to death with his own kitchen knife would be so much better. Yea, I mean REALLY murdering him as soon as he stepped his cheating butt in the door! But guess what? I didn't! Even with all the evidence I had found, he managed to convince me I had it all wrong. He told me of how he had become friends with some girl from work, and my things were moved because he wanted her to think he was single. And although he thought about it, they never had sex. Apparently, I was causing so many issues between us he reached out to someone else for support. Oddly enough, I knew I was right but I chose to believe him! I took full responsibility for him almost cheating on me. That just goes to show how much in love I was with this guy. He couldn't possibly cheat on me because I didn't want him to be cheating. I stayed with him that night and we made love as if nothing had ever happened.

    I tried to do better. I started taking Benadryl to help me sleep some. I got up and got dressed every day. I went online looking for things to do. I started writing poems, songs, and even a short story. I read my Bible and prayed. I prayed a lot. I didn't want to lose him, even though I was perfectly fine with losing myself. I needed to be what he wanted. I became obsessed with trying to please him. I started getting my nails done, wearing the heels he bought for me, you know fixing myself up more. I even wore makeup sometimes and dresses, all of which I wasn't a fan of. I had never been a girly girl. I was quite content with my jeans, sneakers and boots. But he wanted more, so I tried to be more. I even found someone to confide in about the issues I was having. I was trying to work on myself, mostly for him but some for me, too. I didn't like being sad all the time. I was tired of all the highs and lows, the mood swings and crying. I tried, but I couldn't shake the feeling that something was wrong. Then one night my phone rung and the voice on the other end was Seven's. I waited for him to say something and when he did, I realized he wasn't talking to me. I guess he had accidently dialed me without knowing it, so I listened. I heard a child's voice, then that of a woman. I couldn't make out what she was saying, but they seemed very familiar. I hung up immediately and tried calling him with no answer. When we did speak later, he explained that away too ad I believed him…again!

    Time passed and I still couldn't shake the nagging feeling that he was cheating. Of course, he continued to deny it and blame it on my paranoia and insecurities. Although I struggled with it, I chose to continue to have faith in him but not completely. Call me crazy, but I felt God was trying to tell me something. No, it wasn't crazy because God was telling me something. I just knew He was! They don't call it women's intuition for nothing. That is a

God-given instinct that is put in place to let women know when something is off. By this time, I knew without a shadow of a doubt that Seven was cheating, but I had no way of proving it. He continued to be romantic, pop-up visits, little gifts here and there. But there was definitely a shift in his behavior. We had been together nearly four years and I had learned his patterns. He didn't always answer when I called. And in the past, if he missed a call he called back soon after, not now. Sometimes we went all day without talking, which was highly unusual for us. The sweet little text had almost stopped completely. Yet and still he denied that anything was wrong. When he stopped complaining about me not wanting to have sex, I was convinced for sure. Now that little voice in my ear was growing louder and much harder to ignore. Then one day out of the clear blue I just said, "I know you're cheated on me and she just left your apartment." And just like that he confessed.

To say I was devastated would be a huge understatement. How could something I already knew rip my heart to shreds is beyond me. You would have thought I would have prepared myself, but there was no preparing for this. And there it was again that familiar rage that overtook me like a flood. I don't know which was worse, the pain of him being with another woman, the millions of lies, or the fact that he had convinced me to ignore the voice screaming at me that he was cheating. I was so angry, but at myself more than him. I wasn't paranoid! I wasn't crazy! And regardless of what he said it wasn't all my fault. I had given him so many opportunities to leave me, but he wouldn't let go. He didn't have to cheat, he chose to. I immediately ended the relationship and broke all ties with him. I wanted mothing to do with him and had no intention of ever seeing him again. He left his apartment that day for fear of me coming to hurt him. Believe me, that was my first thought but my second thought was my babies. I couldn't do anything that would take me away from them no matter how bad I wanted to cut his penis off and chop it to pieces. I allowed myself to completely fall apart, yet again but this time it didn't last nearly as long. I only told a few people what happened. The truth is I didn't know how long he had been cheating or why I still loved him so very much. But I didn't let him know that. I was as cold as ice. He called and I didn't answer. He texted with no reply. And if I did speak to him, I yelled, screamed, cursed and cried. I was done…until I wasn't.

So, let's wrap this up. God told me some time ago that Seven was my husband, not only that Seven had told me that God assured him that I was his wife. If not for any other reason than that, I couldn't just walk away from him. After a few months, I took him back. Some say I should have made him suffer a while longer, but I waited as long as I could. I was so in love with him and there was no denying that. Being apart from him wasn't only punishing him, but it was killing me. Only a select few knew what had gone down between Seven and me, so transitioning him back in my life wasn't too hard. The girls had no idea we had split until I told them years later. I thought it important to keep my family (especially my girls) and friends out of what was going on just in case we worked things out, which we did. But things were never the same after we got back together.

I can honestly say I had forgiven him, but forgetting was another case entirely. Different scenarios of what could have happened and what he may have done with this other woman played like a bad Lifetime movie in my mind. It didn't help that he refused to give the answers I wanted. It was like I was expected to accept that he cheated, forgive and forget it, and let it go as it had never happened. Well that wasn't working for me at all. I needed to know details. I needed to know just how much of himself had he given to this woman? And was it just one woman, or multiple women? And how long was this going on? When? How? Why? And who? Yea, I wanted to know everything but he gave me nothing, as far as I'm concerned. So, I worked on getting past it, focused on our family and how much I loved him. Even after all this, I still wanted to be his wife. And for some crazy reason, I figured that's the least he could do after how badly he had hurt me. Nope, that wasn't even a thought in his mind.

You would think marriage would be the furthest thing from my mind after he had already shown me what he was capable of. I didn't trust him anymore. There was a constant doubt each time he didn't answer the phone, or took too long to reply to a text. Sometimes we were together, he would leave his phone on silent or wouldn't answer if it rang. I always wondered if it was her reaching out to him. But I never went through his phone. I was no typically the type of woman who went rambling through a man's things looking for evidence. I didn't have the time or the eye power for all that. I was a pretty trusting person UNTIL given a reason not to trust. Whenever he wasn't with me, I wondered if he was with her. It was too much. Add all that to the fact that he still hadn't proposed. Yep, I was rapidly losing patience. Every little box he gave me, I held my breath as I opened it expecting a ring…but no ring. I was starting to feel stupid and like I was a bigger fool than I already thought I was. I will give him this much, he tried his very best to reassure me. He was with us as much as he could be. We talked often when he wasn't there. He showered me with gifts and words of affirmation. We even took family pictures. It was almost like it was when we first met. But there was a noticeable difference for me, the trust wasn't coming back. I didn't trust him with my heart or with my body. The desires I had for him had shifted. I still loved him with all my heart but that thing that drew us together, it was no longer there. We were no longer in agreement about how our relationship should move forward. I wanted to get married and he felt pressured. Neither of us were happy but no one would let go. The thing is we truly loved each other. I personally had never experienced a love so unconditional. Even after all we had been through my heart was still completely tied up in his, and his, mine. But after six years, I needed something more. I was no longer content on being someone's girlfriend. I felt as if I had aged out of that position. I decided if he hadn't proposed by my 35th birthday, I was going to let it go…and that's exactly what I did.

Chapter Fourteen
After Seven

Letting go of the love of my life was one of the hardest and most painful things I had ever done. I knew that someone had to make a move and since Seven wasn't willing to it, that only left me. I had become so exhausted with giving myself away, trying to convince him to marry me, and trying to get things right with God that I just didn't have any fight left. He didn't understand why I walked away when things seemed to be going so well. I honestly couldn't explain it to him, not in a way that he would understand. This is where our age difference came into play. I believe he felt like he had all the time in the world and I felt like I didn't. I wanted more for myself and for my daughters. They deserved a real family and if he weren't ready, we would just have to be a family of three. I let him know he was still welcomed to see the girls and spend as much time with them as he liked. I wasn't trying to take them away from him or hurt him in any way. I didn't end things to force him into proposing either, although I believe that's what he thought. I honestly felt we were never going to get to marriage, and love wasn't enough to make me stay to see if I were wrong. In my heart, I truly believed we would find our way back to each other one day.

As for me, I did my best to pick up the pieces and go on with the business of living. Was it hard? Oh, boy was it ever hard! There were days when I thought I had made the biggest mistake of my life, and then there were others when I felt I should have walked away a long time ago. The one thing I knew for sure is that I couldn't continue to look for my happiness inside someone else. Okay, let's be real, my happiness couldn't be found inside of any man. And it was about time I figured that out. I had to learn how to face the broken-hearted little girl that lived inside of me, help her find healing, and set her free. I had no clue how I was going to do that, but I knew it had to be done. I had spent so many years searching for myself inside of some man, any man. I thought my happiness, my purpose, my worth was in him, but I had it all wrong. I had to find a way to keep the darkness away and let in a little inner light. We all are supposed to have a little light, right?

The first thing I did was enroll in college. I always wanted to earn my bachelors and so it was time that I got that done. The college was right down the street from our apartment, so getting there wouldn't be too hard. However, I was petrified of taking the bus for fear that I may end up somewhere I didn't intend on being. I had lost so much vision by now that I couldn't read street signs or even the numbers on the bus. What if I got on the wrong bus? Or what if I didn't know when or where to get off? I had a counselor who tried to teach me how to maneuver the bus route. She even rode a couple of times with me. Nevertheless, I was too scared to try alone, so I opted to use the dial-a-ride system. It picked me up and dropped me off. I had to wait for long periods of time, but at least I knew I would get to where I wanted to be eventually.

Converse College was an all-girls school which was a good thing for me. I certainly didn't need any manly distractions walking around. It felt good being back in school, it gave me a sense of purpose. I knew this time around would be harder than before. It had been six years since I finished my associates and my eyes had taken a beating. I knew my vision had decreased even more since, then but I didn't care. I had to finish what I started. I always wanted to be Dr. Liquinita Callaham, and although I might not make it quite that far I was determined to at least try. College also gave me a chance to socialize with other people besides my children. They had become my everything after Seven and I ended. So, it was nice to meet and get to know other people. But it was a little hard. I was guarded and had some major trust issues. Besides, I wasn't there to make friends, right? But I sure could use a few. However, education was my priority.

I chose to major in psychology for various reasons. I had always been interested in the way the human mind works. Why do people do the things they do? Why do we all do things differently? What connection is there to our mental processes and our physical reactions to them? You know stuff like that. However, I became more attentive as I watched Alexis grow and change. Her reactions to her visual disability at various stages in her life truly fascinated me. Not to mention, I didn't think there was much focus on how being visually impaired could hugely impact you mentally and emotionally. I remembered how losing my vision had changed the way I felt about myself. I was feeling so many different emotions that varied from day to day, fear, disappointment and anger to name a few. I had no one to talk me through these feelings. I wanted to be that someone for a person going through what I had went through. I tried my best to be that someone for my daughter and other young people like her who were living with blindness or visually impairments. Honestly, I just liked helping people and a degree in psychology would better equip me to do that more effectively.

I eventually mastered the Sparta Bus System! I was so proud of myself. It made getting back and forth quicker and easier. I absolutely loved being in school. I was learning so much! There was always some test to cram for, group project or a paper to write. I enjoyed every bit of it, but it was extremely hard. I do believe I was the only legally blind or blind student on the entire campus. There had to be special accommodations put in place for me. For instance, I was given my notes in large print, closed-circuit televisions in certain classes for magnification purposes, some materials were in audio, and I was given extra time to take tests. There were a lot of people from students to staff ready and willing to assist me. I even had a personal note taker in certain classes. I was also allowed to use a recorder for lectures. And of course, there was a lot of homework and reading; my eyes would get so blurry that I could barely see at times. There were times, as much as I wanted to finish, that I thought about quitting. I didn't want to lose the sight I had left. In fact, I was terrified of losing my sight. Nevertheless, quitting wasn't an option for me. I had two daughters who were watching me and I needed to show them that I could do this, especially Alexis. I didn't want to let them down. More than anything I wanted this for me. I needed it!

Poppa

There was a man in my life that no one knew about. We were rarely ever seen together out in public. He was the person I ran to when all hell was breaking loose in my life, my rock, and my secret place. He was a well-known guy with great ties to the community. He was big on public service efforts and volunteering his time to help those less fortune, a man of prestige and authority. And boy was he a charmer; he could charm the skin off a snake. I'm telling you, he was just that good. He never met a stranger, and he was always willing and waiting to help someone. Everyone knew him, he was loved and well respected in his community. He was so intelligent, but not just in a "book smart" kind of way but just factual. He knew enough about everything to teach you something. He was also wise, and I'm thinking a lot of that wisdom came from his own life experiences. Or maybe also from his unique, spiritual relationship with God. He had a way of looking at things that most Christians probably wouldn't agree with.

Whatever the case, that didn't stop people from coming to him for advice, support or encouragement. He truly was a lot of different things to a mass of people, but to me he was just Poppa.

I can't quite recall when Poppa came into my life, but he became a very important part of it. It's like I looked around one day and he was there filling a space that had never been occupied by anyone. And his presence was so strong that I felt him even when he wasn't around. I loved him instantly (if that's even possible); from the moment he hugged me, I knew that there was something special about him. I just couldn't remember not loving him, it was like I had always loved him, always been connected to him in some sort of way. I was drawn to him in a way that was oddly comfortable and familiar to me. I was able to say anything to him and there was no judgement. I was allowed to be this open, raw version of myself with him with no apologies. He knew my deepest fears and he helped me through them. It was like he saw me as this beautiful wounded bird and he just wanted to help me fly freely again. It was a wonderful feeling having someone in my life that called me on my mess, encouraged me through my struggles, and cared for me without any limitations or expectations. I cherished my relationship with him. I learned how to trust and depend on him, probably a bit too much. He was exactly what I needed at this time in my life where I felt so lost.

Poppa came to visit whenever the girls were away. We sat and talked for hours. He listened to me go on and on about school, the girls, and Seven. We talked about Seven a lot and how much I still loved and missed him so. He helped me to understand things from a man's point of view. Although he never once justified Seven's cheating, he did however help me to see why he may have. He also understood why I had to let him go. I told him about the shadow guys in my life, the ones that I talked to and even went out with but never introduced to family or friends. They never reached that level of importance because I didn't allow them to. Sometimes I buried my face in his chest and cried. I still carried so much hurt inside over so many things and he was the one person I felt most comfortable sharing it all with. He made it easy because he didn't want anything from me, which was good because I had nothing to give. He held me close and let me cry it out. I felt safe there, safe enough to pour my heart out to him and he listened. It takes a special kind of guy to hold a woman while she's crying over another man, but he was just that guy. Sometime I thought I told him too much but it was like word vomit when I was with him, I just couldn't help myself. He didn't seem to mind at all. I did my best to be his safe place, too. He talked to me about various things he was going through, mostly about how unhappy he was with his life and how much he needed a change. Every so often, it was my turn to hold him while he cried. It was those moments that bonded us.

    I remember the first time he kissed me, not like the forehead kiss he gave as he was leaving, I mean the "I see you as a woman" kiss. I was so taken off guard I stood there dumbfounded for a moment. When I finally came to myself, he had already driven off. I didn't know what to make of it since I didn't think we saw each other that way. Things were made clearer when he kissed me again one night while we were sitting on the couch. He drew me into a long, deep, passionate, breath-taking kiss. As soon as the air returned to my lungs, I immediately ran to the bathroom and closed the door. What was going on? What was he thinking? How did I totally misread what was happening? I didn't come out until I heard the front door close. I didn't know what to do. I knew we had gotten close, maybe too close, apparently way too close. I didn't want what was sure to come next. I put some distance between us. I didn't want to ruin the friendship we had established; it was important to me and I didn't want to lose it. He later apologized for crossing the line between us. I accepted his apology, but I couldn't get the moment out of my head.

Poppa had this way of making me see things from his point of view when needed. Some would call it manipulation, but I didn't see it that way. By this time, he didn't have to try very hard to get me to come around to his way of thinking. Truth is, I trusted him completely. I just figured he had never given me a reason not to and I knew he had my best interest at heart. I would do absolutely anything for him. I was drawn to his spirit. I felt connected to him and I loved him just that much! You could say I was vulnerable or gullible or needy, or just plain stupid.

I'm not sure which it was. All I knew is that I liked who I was when I was with him. I was happy! I liked having him around, spending time with him or just hearing his voice on the other end of my phone. He was someone I didn't want to lose. Even though things were becoming complicated between us, I still cherished all the purest parts of our friendship. I wasn't ready to give that up. He helped me see God differently. I desperately needed to see God differently because at the rate I was going, I was sure I was on a slow fall to the deepest pits of hell. Let me explain.

See, up unto this point, I was my own worst critic. I judged myself so harshly for all the things I did wrong. So much so that I had convinced myself that every bad thing that had happened to me was a direct result of a sin that I had committed. I was afraid all the time, afraid that if I did one more thing wrong that God would be done with me forever. More than that, my fear led me to believe that if I kept doing the same wrong thing over and over again, God would send me straight to hell with no questions asked. I thought God was furious with me. I thought he was tired of me asking for forgiveness for the same sin so he wasn't forgiving me anymore. I had begun to put so many rules and stipulations on myself that were impossible to live with but I kept trying. I begged God for one more new chance every time I did something wrong with the vow of never doing that something again…until I did. It was a cycle that went on for years. I sinned, I repented, God forgave me, I didn't forgive myself and I sinned some more. I just wanted to stop disappointing God so all the bad crap in my life would stop happening. I didn't want God to hate me as I thought He did, so I hated myself. I was a spiritual mess, until Poppa helped me see that it was okay to forgive myself and let it go. And that God wasn't the monster that I had made Him out to be.

Poppa also believed in love without limits. There should be no boundaries on who we loved, how we chose to love them, or our expression of that love. For him that meant he should be free to give and receive love from as many women as he chose without any explanation to any of them. For example, if he was in a loving committed relationship with one woman and happened to fall in love with another because she may fill a different need in his life, that should be perfectly fine with all parties involved. He believed that no one person could possibly fulfill all the needs and desires of another; therefore, there should be room for multiple loving relationships with the opposite sex if one desired. Now, I don't know if I agreed with all of that, but some of it made sense to me. I'm not sure where I fit in with all of this for him. I just took it to mean that he was free to love me however he saw fit and should be allowed to express it in whatever manner he chose. Oddly enough, I didn't have a problem with any of it as long as it meant I could have him in my life.

Poppa and I remained close for a very long time. We talked almost every day and saw each other as often as we could. The awkwardness from the kiss had passed and everything was back as it had been before. I did try to stop falling apart so much when he was around. I tried to talk less and listen more because he had a lot going on as well. He often told me how much I meant to him and how he hoped that we would always be close. I didn't think that was much to ask for because I didn't see my life without him in it. I also knew that if I were to get involved with someone else, they were going to have to accept him as a part of my life, although I knew that wouldn't be an easy ask of any guy. But I wasn't there yet, so it didn't matter. Poppa and I embraced what we were given and were grateful for that. However, it was short-lived. One day while he was there for a visit, I was having one of my moments and I'm sure it had something to do with Seven. Anyway, he kissed me again and this time I willingly and fully returned the advance. Then, things took off like a rocket. The next thing I knew we were in the middle of this highly intense sexual encounter. I didn't even remember changing locations and before I realized what was happening it was over. There was nothing loving or passionate about it, it was more lustful and a releasing of sexually frustration. To prove that I wasn't totally freaked out, I remember sitting up and saying "Thank You."

    Call me crazy, and you probably think I am. It didn't change anything between us. It happened, it was over, and we went on. We talked about it a few times, not so much as to analyze the how's and why's but to determine if it should or would happen again. One conversation got detailed when he stated how I should be on call if he wanted to have sex or different ways could do it. We discussed having code words to text if either of us wanted the other for sex. We talked about having sexual escapades in different places and even with other people. It was crazy because I thought about it for a minute. Maybe sex was all I needed because relationships obviously weren't working out. Besides he would do anything for me, give me whatever I needed, and I would still have a wonderful friendship. It didn't sound like a bad deal to me. What did I have to lose? Most of all my heart would be protected because as much as I loved him, it was strictly as a friend.

Well of course, I didn't go through with it. As appealing as it sounded at the time, it just wasn't who I wanted to be. Not to mention the whole God aspect. I hadn't totally given up on my salvation yet. I figured I would eventually get it together. Making the right choice in that moment was a small step in the right direction. Besides I know all sins are the same in the eyes of God, but as far as I was concerned, fornication was one thing but adultery was something else entirely!

Jersey Boi

I want to start by saying I did not go looking for any type of relationship after Seven. I knew I wasn't in the right frame of mind for that, not to mention I was still in love with him. So, I knew getting involved with someone else would be completely unfair to them as well as me. I was focused on the girls and finishing school. I didn't have time for anything else. Therefore, when Jersey came into my life, I stood firmly on my intentions to not get involved. Oddly enough, he respected my position and didn't push the issue at all. He was a nice, Christian guy who appeared to have his head on straight. He was devoted to his relationship with God, so he had his own boundaries in place. He was wicked handsome in a distinguished-gentlemen kind of way. I enjoyed his company. He was easy to talk to and he made me laugh. It felt good to laugh. He had a very kind spirit about him and he was quite helpful to me. As a matter of fact, it was him that taught me how to navigate the Sparta Bus System. I was grateful for his friendship.

But leave it to me to go and mess things up. I still had my "daddy issues" even more so after my relationship with Seven ended. I craved male attention; it made me feel good about myself. Seven still held my heart and I was okay with that. As far as I was concerned, we were divine soulmates and would be back together soon enough. In the meantime, I figured why not indulge in a little taste testing while I waited. I was honest with Jersey about how I felt about Seven which made him quite reluctant to get involved with me. I understood that he wanted a relationship and I wasn't in the heart position to give him that. So, he decided to pursue someone else. He had every right to do so, right? Right! But no, I had to get all wrapped up in my feelings when he stopped talking to me. I didn't want to lose the attention he was giving me. I liked him liking me, whether I wanted to date him or not didn't matter. I went out of my way to make him notice me.

I remember this one time I showed up at his apartment in attempts to seduce him with no intentions of having sex with him. I just wanted him to want me. Stupid and dangerous, yeah, I know! It didn't work though, and I left there feeling even more rejected. I should have just left him alone right then because the complicated drama that followed could have been avoided and omitted from this book.

I think it's important to stress that my god sister warned me not to go down this Jersey shore, but nope I didn't listen. Fast forward a little bit, Jersey and I got close after he ended things with the other woman. We talked a lot, getting to know each other and all that. I felt it necessary to be completely honest about everything, who knew it would be used against me later. So, he knew about all my past relationships, involvements, reckless behavior, and guyships in my life. Thing is, I didn't care what I told him or how he felt about it all. I didn't have anything to hide and I owed him nothing. As we spent more time together, I began to notice that he had some insecurities and trust issues, but it wasn't a big deal because so did I. Then, there were subtle little changes that were flashing red lights that I totally ignored.

Jersey had a serious issue with my guy friends. There were certain guys that had been in my life for years and nothing intimate had ever happened between us, but he didn't trust that. He said there's no way that men and women could be "just friends."

So, he didn't always like it when I talked to them on the phone or if they stopped by for a visit. He always thought that there was more going on than I was telling him. Essentially, he thought I was lying when I said we were just close friends. He didn't like when I wore certain things. He would get agitated if I didn't answer the phone when he called or didn't call back fast enough. I just thought he liked me and didn't want to share me. I didn't realize there was a developing pattern of behavior that I should have been paying attention to. We argued over these things from time to time, but we always worked it out. However, I soon learned he had quite the temper with a silver bullet tongue. Who knew words could hurt worse than any hand ever could?

I take full responsibility for introducing sex into the already complicated relationship. According to him, we were in a committed relationship whereas I felt like we were just dating casually. Needless to say, I shouldn't have been involved in either. But there was this deep need to STILL want someone to want me, the feeling that I got just from being desired somewhat pacified the hole I had inside of me. Jersey wanted to be with me, but he didn't want to have sex with me. That made absolutely no sense to me. Again, my twisted thinking figured those two things went hand in hand. You couldn't have one without the other, not as far as I was concerned. I took his rejection of sex as a personal rejection of me. Should I have known better by this point? Yep, but I didn't! I didn't understand why he didn't want to sleep with me. Well, I take that back. I knew perfectly well why he wasn't interested in having sex and it had nothing to do with me. He told me many times he wanted to wait until marriage or at least a serious committed relationship. I didn't care I needed my fix, that high of having someone intimately connected to me which filled the gnawing ache I carried since a little girl. Eventually, he gave that to me, not just the sex itself but the feeling that came afterward. That, "you're special," feeling or the, "He thinks I'm beautiful" feeling or better yet a combination of the two. Never mind what this all meant for him.

I believed Jersey cared about me, in fact I know he did, which is how I justified his sometimes-irrational behavior. I remember the very first time he hit me with his words. We were outside having a heated discussion about the status of our involvement and I didn't respond the way he thought I should. He called me a "Psychotic bitch." Those words hit me like an eighteen-wheeler with no brakes traveling at maximum speed down a steep hill. I had been called a "blind bitch" a couple of times throughout the years, but never a psychotic one and never by a man. I was devastated; you would have thought he punched me in the face. He might as well have as bad as it hurt. I cried every time I thought about it. I couldn't believe he said that to me. I was trying very hard to be what he needed and not make him mad at me. Somewhere along the way I started to care about him. I cared more than I had intended to, so I didn't like him being mad at me. I didn't want to hurt him. I wanted to make him happy so he wouldn't leave me.

I can't discount the good times we shared. When things were good, they were great. We spent time together watching movies and having dinner. He was a great cook. Sometimes, we would go for a long walk and just talk. He tried his best to be there when I needed him. If I asked him for something, he would get it for me. He was good about making sure I had what I needed. There were times when he walked me to the bus stop in the cold and waited with me until the bus came. Other times when I stepped off the bus from school, he waited to walk me home. There were surprise lunches and little tokens he gave me for no reason at all. And of course, I can't forget how he would leave me love songs on my social media page. It was all so sweet and I truly appreciated the effort. Like I said, he was a good guy with a good heart. But someone had hurt him badly in the past and I was paying the price for it.

I was so upset over what was happening that I decided to talk to my mother, which led to a whole other series of events. That's another story altogether. After the "bitch" incident, I immediately cut him off and returned all his gifts. This should have been the point where I walked away completely but for the life of me, I can't explain why I didn't. After a few months and what seemed to be a heartfelt apology, we were back at it again.

I started changing. I felt the change but it's like I was powerless to stop it. I became a liar. I lied to myself about what was happening. I lied to my girls when I told them that his behavior towards me was completely my fault. I lied to him when I said I could do better and be the type of woman he wanted. I lied to the people closest to me when I pretended everything was alright. If you were to ask him, he would say I was always lying. But all I was trying to do was not make him upset with me, which I managed to do no matter what I did. I stopped wearing certain things. I stopped talking to certain people. I stopped being me. I was having trouble in school, my grades were slipping, and I just couldn't seem to get it together. All I was concentrated on is making sure he wasn't mad at me. All this for a guy that I knew I wasn't supposed to be dealing with. Yea, I grew to care about him a lot, but that's just the kind of person I am. I care about people even if they hurt me, treat me bad and I couldn't stand for someone to be mad at me. I was in a mess and I didn't know how to get out.

I was a bitch a lot over the next year or so, a stupid one, a lying one, an ugly one, and a whorish one. Every time I looked around, I was doing something wrong, talking to a guy on the bus, not calling enough, posting on Facebook, misreading something he said…it was always something and it was always my fault. There were times that he cut me off completely and I should have let him walk away, but I couldn't. It was something about him that I felt as if I HAD to have him. Besides, the rejection was too much to bare. I couldn't stand seeing him with someone else. And so, we would eventually find ourselves together again. Other times I tried to walk away, but I kept going back telling myself it was my fault that he got so angry. It was my fault because I hurt him, by letting him invest his feelings when I knew I couldn't return them the way he deserved. I owed it to him to stay because I shouldn't have gotten involved with him in the first place. It was my fault that he hung up on me, slammed the door in my face, called me names and cursed me out in the middle of the street. This is my punishment for playing with someone's feelings! I deserved all of it!

It became a vicious, dysfunctional cycle of mental and emotional abuse. I did something wrong, he broke me down with his words, I apologized, he forgave me and we started all over again. Now I will be the first to admit that I caused a lot of issues between us. I knew what he wanted from me from the start and I knew I wasn't equipped to be what he needed. I will admit that. I should have left him alone. I should have never had sex with him. My selfishness caused him to be hurt and his response was to hurt me back as much as I hurt him. His words were lethal and they accomplished their intended mission. I hated myself, my eyes, my scars, my body, my hair…I hated it all. I couldn't find one good thing about myself. I didn't think I was worth anything. The little self-esteem that I had managed to build was shattered by this point. I couldn't continue to allow my girls to see me like this. I needed them to know that it wasn't okay to let a man or anyone treat you this way. So, after many more highly intense verbal altercations, police involvement, and just sheer exhaustion, I was finally able to walk away.

Questions Unanswered

I had attempted many times to change who I was and learn how to make different choices. I knew it wasn't by chance that the biggest mistakes that I had made were somehow tied to a man. If I wasn't trying to be cool with the popular guy, I wouldn't have been raped at nineteen. Walking into that apartment that day created a moment that changed the course of my entire life. So many bad choices after that, and although there were some wonderful blessings mixed in, something had to give. I couldn't afford to continue making the same wrong choices repeatedly. I needed to do something different, make better choices. I needed to figure out why it seemed that I was happier with a man than without one. I needed to know why acceptance was so important to me. Why did it matter what someone else thought of me? Why was it so hard for me to love and accept myself? What was wrong with me? I knew there had to be a reason and I had a pretty good idea what it was. No, I can't blame every bad decision I have ever made on my absentee father but I have often wondered if by life would have been different if he was a part of it. If you ask me, I would say yes! Others say you can't miss what you never had, but I totally disagree. There was only one person who could help me answer these questions, so it was time to call my father.

I had a long, overdue conversation with my

father. I needed to know why he chose not to be a part of my life. And I needed to hear it from him. It took me quite a few tries to build up the courage to call but I finally did it. I can still remember the sound of his voice. It didn't sound warm and inviting like I thought it should; it sounded like maybe calling him wasn't the best idea. I swallowed the large lump in my throat and said "Hello, this is Liquinita." It irritated me that I had to tell him who I was. He should have known by the sound of my voice or he should have recognized my number on his caller ID. Perhaps that would require regular communication? Even so, I pressed on with the conversation, realizing he knew more about me than I thought he did. This made me feel all warm inside, like her cared enough to want to know about me. He probably got all that information from my brother because he certainly didn't get it from me. As the conversation continued, I felt the warm fuzzy feeling turn into pain and a slow rising anger as I took note of the frustration in his voice. How dare he have the nerve to be frustrated with my questions? He at least owed me that much! Okay, maybe I should have just left well enough alone. Nope, I couldn't, no matter how much it may hurt I had to know why.

    The conversation seemed longer than it was. There were these longs periods of awkward silence, followed by his one-word responses to my questions. It was obvious I wasn't getting anywhere with the small talk so I finally just blurted it out, "Why did you leave me?" The question must have caught him off guard because he snapped back, "What did you say?" So, I asked him again and this time he answered with an explanation that only pissed me off. "Your grandmother told me to stop coming around so I did. It's in the past so just leave it alone. It doesn't matter." I exploded, "What? It doesn't matter! Are you kidding me? It does matter. I needed you! You were my father! Do you have any idea what I have been through? Didn't you know how much I needed you? So, you just never came back? You didn't care how that made me feel? You didn't wonder about me? Why didn't you love me enough to fight for me? Didn't I matter as much as your other children?" Rapid fire, questions one after the other, met with dead silence. I felt the burning in my chest, my eyes watered as the tears prepared to drown my face, but I refused to let them fall. I was not giving him the satisfaction of knowing how much he was hurting me. Still no reply. We sat in silence for what seemed like forever. I finally realized he wasn't going to say anything else, so I said, "Thank you. I love you. Bye."

That was it. The conversation I waited over thirty years to have was over in a matter of minutes. Before there was a place in my heart on reserve just for my daddy and now there was hollowness, a place that would never be filled. I did love him. I had loved him with all my heart for my entire life. I was taught to love him and so I did. My mother never said one bad word about him. As a matter of fact, she often told me that my daddy loved me. I never understood how she could say that about a man who couldn't bother to show up for either of us. I didn't want to love him, but God helped me. I was hurt and angry and even more so after I had this conversation with him. But I still loved him. I came to the realization that day that I would probably always love him. I just had to find a way to be okay with that. Truth is, I wasn't okay with it and I didn't think I ever would be. Is it possible to love and hate someone at the same time? Maybe it wasn't hatred; maybe I was devastated that the one person who I so desperately wanted to love me chose not to. How was I supposed to live with that? I had to find a way to make peace with it, I just didn't know how.

Chapter Fifteen
No Test, No Testimony

    Life has a way of taking unexpected twists and turns. Even when there are road signs warning us of what's ahead, we don't always prepare ourselves for what's just around the bend. This certainly was the case for me when I received an unexpected phone call during the Spring of 2012. My friend on the other end of the phone asked if I was okay. I was fine and I told her. And that's when she dropped the news on me. She told me that Seven had gotten married. The tears flowed almost instantly before I even had a chance to process what she said. I heard the words, but my mind couldn't process them. Needless to say, my heart got the message loud and clear. There was an instant shattering that went to the core of my heart. I don't quite know how to explain the devastation of it all. My body went limp as I crumbled under the weight of what I had just heard. I wept bitterly as if someone had died. But someone had died, me! My heart is the core of who I am and it had just been viciously murdered by the man I loved.

    I remember the day Seven called and asked to see me. I was a little surprised at his request but I was more than willing to see him. Things between us had managed to even themselves out to a place where I considered us to be friends. There was still some residual pain from our breakup, but I managed to push that down to hold on to the bond we shared. It could very well be that I was holding on to any possibility of a future with him. I still loved him deeply, there was no denying that and I knew he loved me just as much. There was no doubt in my mind about that. However, he had a girlfriend at the time and I had no intentions of coming between that. I figured he had to work some stuff out and I would be here waiting for his proposal when he was done. You might say I was in denial but I say I had faith, faith that things would be just as God had intended for us. Anyway, he said he needed to talk to me and I wanted to know what he had to say.

It had been awhile since I had seen him. He still looked just as gorgeous as ever. He had picked up a little weight but he wore it well. When he walked through the door, he took me in his arms and held me like he had done so many times before. All the memories of us came flooding back, it felt so good to be in his embrace. We sat down and he began talking to me about his girlfriend. I listened attentively as he poured his heart out. He talked about the struggles they had and all the things he didn't like as he compared her to me. He also told me about all the wonderful qualities she possessed that made her special. Then he told me how he was making a decision on whether to marry her or end the relationship. Strangely enough, where most women would have taken offense that their ex-boyfriend whom they were still in love with was coming to them for relationship advice, I was not. This was a great opportunity for me to pour out my heart and tell him how much I loved him and wanted him to choose me. Nope, I refused to do that! If he loved me like I thought he did, he was going to have to choose me all on his own. I simply told him not to do to her what he had done with me, "Don't waste her time. If you truly love her, then you should marry her." I truly meant it with all my heart. The thing is I didn't think he loved her enough to marry her, but boy was I wrong!

It hurt. It hurt like nothing I had ever felt in my entire life. The pain was so deep that I could barely catch my breath at times. My heart was shattered and I just knew that it would never be whole again. I don't know what hurt more, the fact that he married someone else or that he didn't tell me himself. In fact, none of the people that I thought would have told me said a word. I guess they thought enough time should have passed that I wouldn't have been impacted. Wrong! I had to see the pictures on social media. To see him touching someone else, kissing someone else, it was too much. Even though I was looking at them, I still couldn't believe it was real. I had to talk to him. I had to hear him say it. And he said it, so it was true! I still couldn't swallow it. It's like I couldn't make my heart see what my mind couldn't understand. How was it possible that the man God said was my husband was now married to another woman? That didn't make any sense at all to me! Why? Why was this happening? I know you're probably thinking, "Well he told you what he was going to do." You're right he did tell what COULD happen, I just didn't think it WOULD.

I spent six years with a man who had become a part of my heart. My very best friend and the person I had planned to spend the rest of my life with was gone. Only two years after we broke up, he managed to give another what I waited years to get. Six years, six years of my life gone and I was left with nothing. What did she do in two years that I couldn't accomplish in six? I was sick with pain. Every time I ate, I vomited. I eventually stopped eating altogether. I wasn't sleeping either. I laid in my bed every night trying to figure out what I did so wrong? How did this happen? Didn't I love him enough? Didn't I encourage and support him enough? I gave him all of me, everything I had even at the risk of losing my relationship with God. I sacrificed everything and this is what I got? What the hell? Who is this woman that could come in and win him over in such a short period of time? Then it hit me, like a bolt of lightning. She wasn't new; she was already there. He had chosen the other woman over me! Now that's when the pain really hit!

I became fixated on this woman who had taken him from me. I wanted to know everything I possibly could about her, like where she worked, where she lived, where she went to school? Did she have kids? How old was she? How long had she and Seven known each other? Whatever there was to know I wanted to know it. I had to! Every free moment I had I spent stalking her social media pages, reading her words, looking at pictures of her and Seven. I looked at every wedding picture there was to see. I zoomed in so I could see every little detail. I did this every single day for months. I was totally obsessed! I needed to know what set this woman apart from me. What was it about her that made her better, chosen by him? Why her and not me? I picked myself apart bit by bit right down to the color of my skin. Truth is, I couldn't compare to her. She was educated, employed, and a driver with two-working eyes. She was everything I wasn't. Just another in-my-face reminder that I just wasn't good enough. I was never good enough.

The Test

It was during the fall of 2012 when my life was forever changed by an unexplainable series of events. I'm writing this in part from the point of view of the observers who walked through this trial with me, considering my memories during this time- period are muddled and hazy. There are parts that I recall so vividly but with questionable validity because it became difficult to decipher imagination from reality. However, the emotions I experienced during this time remained etched in my mind, the hopelessness depression, and sheer desperation to leave this life behind. I didn't imagine that I would ever come out on the other side of what remains a medical mystery.

I opened my eyes to see the tear streaked face of my baby girl. Her beautiful, happy, smiling face was replaced with fear and worry and I had no idea why. I'm sure my mother was there, too, but I can't remember seeing her. Besides, my eyes were locked in on my baby and why she was looking so sad. And where was Alexis? The almost blinding florescent lights shone bright from above, so much so that it was hard to keep my eyes opened. I had no idea how I ended up in this hospital room. The last thing I remembered was walking in the apartment from school, and at some point, I grabbed my keys and walked out the door again. I can't recall where I went or how I got to wherever I ended up. The next thing I knew, I was there, in this hospital bed with no recollection of the events that landed me here. This was just the beginning of a long, frightening journey that changed my life forever.

    I can recall the heaviness in my legs, trying to move them into a more comfortable position but there wasn't one. It was like they were stones; I could still feel them there but moving them took way more effort than it should have. My head pounded like a base drum and there was a weird, ringing echo in my ears. I remember the waterfall of hot tears on my face and the panic in my heart as I laid there wondering what was happening to me. There were doctors and nurses coming in and out of the room talking to me, but I couldn't comprehend what they were saying. My first cousin April was there. She is more like a sister than a cousin. She had recently moved to Spartanburg, which gave us an opportunity to get even closer than we already were. She was doing most of the talking for me. For some reason, although I heard the words clearly in my mind, they weren't coming out of my mouth the same way. It was very frustrating because I knew what I wanted to say but couldn't. I didn't know the answer to simple questions like, what month it was or who was president? The whole experience was terrifying. I had no idea what was going on or why. I just wanted to go home, but I soon learned that wasn't an option anytime soon. Then there was darkness.

    I can't remember how long I was in the hospital or all the things they did to me there. I was told about all the tests taken to try and find out what was wrong, but there were no answers. When I was finally released from the hospital, I was on a walker. I couldn't stand or walk without assistance. My legs were very weak. I was unable to keep my balance without toppling over. I had also lost the ability to speak properly. My words came out jumbled and slurred whenever I tried to speak, which made it hard for others to understand me. I had no memory of the events that caused me to be hospitalized in the first place. I was later told that Alysha and one of my classmates had found me wandering at a shopping center across the street from our apartment complex. Apparently, I had called home confused about where I was. Alysha said by the time they got to me, I was disoriented and didn't recognize her so they called the paramedics. I didn't remember any of that. It was if my memory had a mind of its own and it came and went as it pleased. There were several offered explanations of what may have happened to me, a stroke, seizure, or some type of psychological break, but no definitive answer.

Days turned into weeks as I watched different people come in and out of our home. There were physical therapists, speech therapists, occupational therapists and nurses who came weekly to work with me. I had to learn how to do what used to be familiar things all over again. Things like taking a shower, getting dressed or even getting into bed were difficult and I couldn't do them alone. I couldn't be left alone at all because I started having these seizure-like episodes where my body shook violently without warning. My friends and family took turns staying with me. My grandmother, auntie and mother who had taken leave from work, made up a schedule to come be with me and help take care of my girls. It was all quite overwhelming. The feeling of frustration and complete helplessness started to settle in. I was always able to take care of myself and my children. It was the one thing I took great pride in, my greatest accomplishment, I was a great mother. And now I couldn't do anything.

Things were getting worse. There were many trips to the ER. The "episodes" were increasing and more intense. My body would get ice cold and that seemed to trigger the shaking, but other times the reverse would happen. My legs were like jelly beneath me and they would ache. I had trouble getting them to go. I spent a lot of time lying down or propped up on the couch. My speech would be good at times, but other times you couldn't understand a word I was saying. I started seeing things that weren't there, which not only scared others but totally freaked me out. The worst part of this is that my girls told me I didn't always recognize who they were. I would see them and become afraid because in my mind they were supposed to be younger than they were. I was losing time a lot, huge gaps in my memory. The days seemed to all run together and I wasn't always clear of where I was. And of course, I had to take a medical withdrawal from college for the second time in my life in my senior year. That was devastating to me because I wanted nothing more than to graduate with my Bachelors. I had come so far and I was so close to the end. It hurt; it all hurt because I had no clue what was coming next.

Where was I in all of this? The only way to explain it is like this. I felt like my body was holding me hostage. I could hear, see and feel everything that was happening but I had no control over it. I wanted to scream out to the outside world, "Help me, I'm in here!" but I couldn't make a sound. I was alive in my heart but it felt my mind was crumbling. I couldn't make sense of anything. It was like I was fighting to free myself, but all my defenses were down. I felt unprotected, vulnerable and alone although I was surrounded by people who loved me. In all the things, I had been through, all the things I thought I couldn't survive, all the rejection, hurt and brokenness, and the times I wanted to kill myself, it was now that I prayed for death. I literally begged God to take my life. There was nothing I wanted more than for all of it to end. It was torture. I watched my mother pray for me, my children cry with worry about me. I saw the fear in their eyes. I watched as Alysha stepped up as the little lady of the house, cooking and cleaning after a full day of school. Alexis became my nurse maid, making sure I took all my meds on time and sleeping with me every single night. I laid in bed during my sleepless nights watching her next to me as she tried not to sleep too hard in case, I needed her. I felt their love for me so strongly. It hurt me to see them suffering and there was nothing I could do to make it better.

Over time there were countless tests taken, MRI's, CAT scans, nerve tests, and a lot of blood work.... nothing! The Neurologist couldn't find evidence of anything wrong. Then, it had to be mental. All in my head! Stress, or a psychological problem that manifested into physical symptoms. Really? So, everything that I was going through was caused by me! I was the reason that my body was turning against me? That was crazy, not to mention it pissed me off. Although from my studies on the subject, it could very well be possible. Why was this happening now? And if I was doing this to myself, why couldn't I stop? No, something was wrong! I believe my family adapted the notion that since there wasn't a medical explanation that the psychiatrist must be right.

So now I had to take my psychiatric meds, pray and read the Bible so I could be healed and delivered. Wait, what? Well I wanted no part of that. Did I still have just a little bit of faith left? Yes! Did I still believe in God? Absolutely! But I had nothing to say to my Father. As far as I was concerned, He was responsible for all of this. I became so angry, more than I had ever been in my life. I know that I had done some stuff wrong. I knew that maybe God was disappointed in me, but was this the way he decided to punish me? Did I deserve all of this? Yea, to say I was pretty upset with God would be a gross understatement. If this is how He chose to deal with me, then I was done with Him. I shut down completely.

I was on a lot of different medications, some for my legs, anti-seizure, thyroids, and insomnia to name a few. I'm ashamed to admit this, but I started taking the insomnia pills all the time. When I say all the time, but I mean all day. Whenever I was hurting physically or emotionally, I put myself to sleep. Sometimes I added Benadryl with them to slow everything down; it calmed and relaxed me. I was secretly hoping that the right amount of these meds would kill me. I bet you're thinking if I wanted to die there were other ways to get the job done. I know that's what I thought about people who said "I tried to kill myself." Well in my case, I was a coward who didn't like pain, I didn't want my kids to find a bloody mess, and the pills were all I had access to. I was so tired of feeling trapped inside my body, tired of the pain, the inability to talk, the hallucinations that had started, and the trips to the hospital that ended with no help at all. No one truly understood what I was going through. I just wanted out of this life! I no longer cared about anything or anything else, not even my girls. I was so tired of seeing them hurting. I knew my girls would be taken care of, besides I was no use to them in my current state. Death, all I wanted was death and if I kept taking these drugs then maybe, just maybe I wouldn't wake up.

Death never came and I was a walking zombie. I went from feeling everything to feeling nothing at all. I didn't talk to many people, not only because they couldn't understand me but because I had nothing to say. I didn't want to go anywhere because I was embarrassed being on a walker. Not to mention I never knew when I was going to have one of those "episodes" so I would much rather be at home. I didn't want a lot of people coming over because I didn't want anyone seeing me like this. That didn't stop Seven from coming by after he heard the news. Seeing him, rather having him see me only made things worse. I was less than who I was the last time he saw me. I could see the concern on his face as well as the pity in his eyes. I wondered could he see the pain in mine as I held his left hand in mine starring at the ring on his wedding finger. Now he was someone else's husband. It was one thing to see it in pictures but quite another to see it in person.

I wish I could have found the words to convey the amount of pain I was in, how my heart shattered all over again in that moment. I knew he genuinely cared about me. Perhaps the love he expressed to me was real but I couldn't understand it. Why would someone who claimed to love me so much marry someone else? I didn't know who I felt worse for, her or me! Either way, I didn't want him there, and when he finally left, I cried for hours. I was so discouraged and depressed and I didn't attempt to hide it. Maybe the doctors were right, maybe after everything that I had endured and never truly dealt with, my mind finally broke into unrepairable pieces. Maybe what was happening to me was a direct result of EVERYTHING life had handed me. Maybe this is how it all was going to end. I just didn't care anymore. Every day my only secret prayer was, "God, please just let me die!"

The Testimony

It was almost a year before I started to feel normal again. It took some time, but I eventually got strong enough to stand and then walk on my own. I didn't hurt nearly as bad and those strange seizure-like episodes were happening less and less. I started speaking clearly again, although there were times when the slur returned. It usually happened when I was very tired or stressed out about something. It appeared that a lot of the issues I was experiencing were psychologically related. I was never given a medical explanation for what happened to me. I had a hard time accepting that everything I endured over the past year, everything I'd put my family through, could have all been caused by a mental break. It didn't make sense to me, the pain I felt in my body was real, the inability to walk and talk were out of my control. I lost a huge chunk of my life, so many things

I couldn't remember. I struggled coming to grips with it all.

My girls had grown and changed so much during this time, they had experiences I had no recollection of. I felt I missed out on a whole year of their lives. This crisis had a profound impact on my children, and it changed them. From time to time, the girls would tell me about something that occurred during that year that I have no memory of. It makes me so sad to think of all the things I missed with them. To this very day, they are extremely overprotective of me and fear sets in every time I get sick. Alexis hates leaving me alone for fear of me having an "episode." If there's ever a time she can't find me in the house, she immediately checks on the floor to see if I have passed out because she found me like that once. Alysha calls and checks on me whenever we are apart to make sure I'm okay. And she insists on me resting as much as I can whenever she thinks I have done too much. They worry about me more than any child should have to. And I carry the guilt of doing that to them to this very day. I realize that getting sick wasn't my fault, but my heart carries the responsibility of causing my girls pain. I recently learned that the symptoms I experienced may have been caused by a Thyroid Strom. I had been diagnosed with Hyperthyroidism earlier that year, so basically my thyroid numbers could have been out of whack. The numbers could have been either too high or low, I'm not sure which. Knowing there could be a medical explanation for it all makes me feel better than thinking I lost my mind. Either way, there's no way of knowing now.

That experience was my personal hell on earth. It changed me. There was no way that anyone can tell me that God isn't real. He had to be because there was no other explanation to why I was still alive. The doctors didn't even know what was wrong with me. They concluded it was all in my head. My family thought I was stressed, tired, or that my broken heart had broken my mind. There were others who believed it was a direct attack from Satan. I didn't know what it was. But it was the longest, darkest, loneliest, most painful, depressing frightening time of my entire life. I tried to kill myself more than once but failed. I prayed for death, but God did not allow it. He is the reason t I survived. Every once and awhile, in those darkest times, just when I thought it was over, there was this whisper in my spirit that said, "Hold on, you're going to be alright!" Truth is, I didn't believe it at all and I didn't put up much of a fight either. But God fought for me, He battled me for my life and He won. God saved my life and no one can convince me otherwise.

God continued to show Himself in my life after this. I eventually went back to school. Everyone there was excited for my return and were ready and willing to help in any way they could. And I needed all the help I could get because I struggled. School was already hard for me before because of my visual disability. Now add the fatigue, headaches, and occasional dizzy spells accompanied by my inability to retain information at times. It was a challenge to say the least and I cried almost every day. There were times I would get so overwhelmed and frustrated with myself. Other times, I didn't think I would ever get it all done and just wanted to quit. But I had an extraordinary support system along the way, from Converse staff, my professors, other students, family and friends. My baby girl Alysha probably knows just as much about Psychology as I do considering all the material she read to me. She and Alexis were right there encouraging me all the way. My mother, who had faith that I could accomplish absolutely anything was praying me through. God's mercy and grace proved sufficient for me. With His help, I pushed through and earned my Bachelors of Arts in Psychology from Converse College. The most amazing wonderful part of it all is that Alexis, Alysha and I all graduated together in May of 2014! In fact, the local newspaper *The Spartanburg Herald Journal* featured a story on the three of us, *Upstate family stays together, graduates together*. Look it up, you will find it online. We had come full circle, together and I couldn't have been prouder, happier or more grateful!

Chapter Sixteen
Revelations

It took another failed attempt at a relation for me to finally realize that maybe I should just stop trying. Obviously, I wasn't very good at them. I won't bother going through all the details of who, what and why, but just know it was all his fault. Okay, well maybe not completely, but a good ninety- five percent for sure. Anyway, it was very brief and I won't give him the satisfaction of mentioning him in my story. Take note that I had the good sense to end things before they went too far left. The five percent that belonged to me was the reason I decided not to pursue or accept any more relationships. My heart was healing but my trust was shattered. If it even felt like he was lying to me, I was ready to call it quits. And it didn't help that he gave me plenty of reasons to doubt him. So, before I ended up killing him, it was best to let him go. And as overdramatic as you may think I'm being, I am dead serious. I was sure that if one more man betrayed me, he would have to die. Simple as that! I was done with all the heartbreak and my tolerance was shot. I just couldn't do it anymore. The worst part is, I didn't care. The relationship was over and I could care less. I didn't fall apart or get all depressed. I didn't feel anything, not even disappointment. Nothing!

That was five years ago and I haven't been in a committed relationship since then. Yep, five whole years! Let's just stop and give me a hand for that! I'm proud of myself! However, there have been a few temporary lapses in sexual judgment along the way, one in particular that led to a pivotal turning point in my life. So, I met him online, first mistake. I went to his house alone, second mistake. You can guess what the third mistake was. There were no feelings involved, well at least not on my part. And I didn't feel guilt or regret. It was purely consensual adult extracurricular activity to satisfy lustful fleshly desires. Nothing more. It had nothing at all to do with him but the pleasure he provided was quite addictive. I lost my mind there for a minute. I told you great sex has a way of doing that to you. Though, the real good Christians (you know those who never sin) would say the devil made me do it, but I say I was all me, and my love of great sex. I'm a firm believer in taking responsibility for my actions, and I can't blame the devil for everything. Besides I knew exactly what I was doing. I wanted to get lost in the pleasure for a while, so I did. There is always a cost for ungodly pleasure.

God has always had a way of getting my attention. I didn't always like the way He chose to do it, but I'm sure He didn't like having to do it either. Many people lean to the notion that God doesn't work that way; he doesn't punish us for our sins. I, on the other hand, totally disagree. Besides what kind of parent continues to allow their child to misbehave without consequences or chastisement? Not a very good one, if you ask me. And as I had come to see it,

God was my Father, I was His daughter. He had allowed me to get away with a lot of mess with what I called 'soft spankings." You know, a warning here, a consequence there. God had shown me way more mercy than I ever deserved. Maybe, this time He thought I needed a wakeup call because that's exactly what I got.

I was riding with my girls when I received a call from my Gynecologist who informed me that I had contracted an STD. The nurse told me it wasn't too serious and treatable with antibiotics. That should have made me feel better, but it didn't because now I had to explain this to my girls. They quickly picked up from the tone in my voice that something was wrong. They were my grown little women now and it wasn't so easy to hide things from them. And I had made it a point to always tell them the truth no matter what, especially when they asked a direct question. So, when they asked, "Mommy what did the doctor say?" I couldn't lie to them. With tears in my eyes, I explained to my daughters how I had contracted a STD from having unprotected sex. I was so ashamed of myself. I couldn't imagine what they thought of me, the disappointing look of disgust on their faces said it all.

Yet, it was just the jolt I needed to change my life. I had been living a life of insanity, just doing the same destructive things repeatedly, expecting something different to happen…and it never did. It was time to take a long hard look at myself. I needed to set a better example for my girls. I never wanted to see them look at me like that again. I wanted better for myself, too. I wanted to experience true inner peace and happiness. I finally realized that there wasn't a man alive that could give that to me. I also knew I couldn't accomplish that on my own, I needed God. I had been dragging Him along behind me for years, picking Him up and putting Him down whenever it was convenient. He had to be tired of me because I was tired of myself. I was ready to surrender it all to Him, the years of rejection, insecurity, and hidden shame that I couldn't seem to shake. I was just too exhausted to keep going the way I had been. I had to change, there was no other option or my soul would surely die. That was two years ago, and I haven't entertained a man in any way whatsoever, no relationship, no dates, and absolutely NO SEX! I finally, and I mean completely totally and for real finally stopped searching.

Father

It was the day of my 40th birthday party and I was so excited to be celebrated with my best friend whose birthday was ten days after mine. But before we got to celebrate, we were going to attend my little brother's wedding. I was nervous about going. I had changed my mind a few times, but ultimately decided I couldn't miss it. I knew it was important to him for me to be there, but I don't think even he knew what it would cost me. The wedding was beautiful and I should have left as soon as it was over. However, my best friend convinced me to stick around a little to congratulate my brother and his new bride, so I agreed. I sat on a pew and waited as the wedding party took pictures. Then the photographer called for all my father's children to take a family picture. I sat and watched as three brothers and one sister with smiling faces crowded around my father for the picture. I sat there stone-faced, refusing to allow even one tear to fall as I watched them watch me as they took one happy picture after another. My father didn't bother to acknowledge my presence. It's almost like he looked right through me. They all did, but it was my father who I blamed for it all.

I was instantly dragged back in time to every birthday, Christmas, hospital stay and every other daddy moment he missed. I felt hot tears boiling in my eyes as I tried to swallow the mountain of pain in my throat that was threatening to choke me to my death. The reality of the moment hit me like a derailed freight train traveling full speed ahead. I fought to catch my breath without showing an ounce of emotion. I refused to allow any of them to see my pain. It was his rejection in that moment that told the truth that I refused to acknowledge. He wanted absolutely nothing at all to do with me. He had chosen his family and I wasn't a part of it. I decided that would be the final slap in the face rejection that my father would ever give me. I got up, walked out, and when I got it the car, I let it go. I wept bitterly for I don't know how long. It hurt so bad; it left this indescribably soul-crushing pain that rocked my body to its core. But I promised myself that day that He would never hurt me like that again.

It took a very long time, fervent prayers and a whole lot of tears to get past the pain of that day. And although I have gotten passed it, I still carry it with me. I will never forget the pain of such an open rejection from a man that was supposed to love me. Every time I think of that moment, I cry. Actually, as I am writing this, I'm suddenly right back there in that church watching the family pictures, it hurts, and the tears are falling. It's hard to believe that a person who was never a part of my life could impact it in such a way. Truth is, I have been waiting for the day that I just didn't care about my father but it has never come. As a matter of fact, he had a medical crisis some time ago and I decided to reach out to him. At first, the communication was slow but as time passed it improved. We rarely ever speak on the phone but I make sure to text him at least once a week to check on him. Sometimes the text can go on for a while. He may talk to me about his health or things that have happened in his past life. Sometimes I ask him questions and he will answer, other times he won't. I know not to push too hard. There are times his responses are short and sharp, and he will cut the conversation off. He has never expressed any interest in me, my life, his grandchildren or anything else concerning me. I have learned to take what he offers and not ask for anything more. Besides, what we have is more than I thought I would ever have.

Our text message relationship is sufficient for me. I've accepted that I most likely won't get any more than that. And I'm okay with it. I no longer have an intense need for him. I don't need him nor do I want him to have an active role in my life anymore. That time has finally passed and I'm so grateful it has. I finally realize that who I am has nothing at all to do with who he is or what he's done for me. That took some time to swallow, too. However, I still struggle with the fact of him not acknowledging me as his daughter, although he has never denied being my father when I asked him. He has never acknowledged he's my father to all my siblings, which has caused a whole other set of issues. I don't appreciate what his refusal to acknowledge me implies about my mother. I know my mother would never lie to me and if there was a possibility of someone else being my father, she would have told me. She's just not deceitful in that way or any other way. I feel like he has placed a dark cloud of doubt over my head that follows me wherever I go. I can't seem to get away from the gnawing feelings of wanting to be accepted by him. It's no longer about WHO I am as much as it is about WHOSE I am. Conflicting emotions reside in me concerning him but none of them will allow me to discard him or hate him. And there are times when I feel hating him would be much easier than loving him. I want to see him well, happy, and living a good life even though he has hurt me more than any other man ever has or possibly could.

Pops
An Answered Prayer

Have you ever been given an unexpected gift? It was something you've always wanted but never thought you would actually obtain. Well that's what Pops was to me, a beautiful surprise. When he and my mother married, I always figured he was God's gift to her. And I was perfectly fine with that because I loved seeing her so happy. But as far as I was concerned there was nothing, he could offer me. It wasn't because he didn't try but because I just refused to let him in. I had enough daddy issues without adding him to the list. I couldn't allow myself to long for something from someone that I could never have. I couldn't take the disappoint nor could my heart take the rejection of yet another man. But Pops wasn't just any ole man, he was special. He was genuinely good and kind with no effort needed. He was a true gentleman, the kind that rarely exist anymore. He was soft spoken, never raised his voice not even when he was angry (I rarely saw him angry). But he was firm in speech when need be. He was a hard worker and could build just about anything. He was respectful and well respected, everyone knew him. He was a faithful man of God who believed in family and old-fashioned values. He wasn't perfect at all but as close to it as I had ever seen.

I didn't come easy, yea I liked him well enough for my mother but I never considered him for myself. My mother must have seen something in him that I didn't pick up right away because she tried her best to get me to see what she saw. I remember I would call home to talk to her sometimes and every single time before we hung up, she would say, "You wanna speak to your daddy?" Then she would giggle. It used to make me so mad because he wasn't my daddy and I didn't have much to say to him. He knew it was hard for me but he made it easier with his kindness and gentleness towards me. We would get on the phone per my Mother's request and exchange pleasantries. Somewhere in those brief conversations he would let out this contagious laugh that was so warn and sweet that it just melted my heart. Before long I was laughing too. He respected my space and didn't force himself on me. He was so patient with me and I know I didn't make it easy. I was never mean or rude or anything, I was just extremely guarded where daddies were concerned. But he didn't seem to notice at all, he continued to be his naturally loving self. Before I knew it, our little conversations were not so little. We began talking more without my mother's urging. W called each other all the time and we couldn't reach me he would leave the funniest voice mails. We started to form our own special bond. As times passed, we got to be very close and he slowly and subtly eased his way into my heart. I can't even remember when he went from Mr. David to Pops because the transition was just that smooth.

    I eventually left Spartanburg and moved back to McCormick with my parents. Notice I said, "Parents." Yea, I had let him in alright! It wasn't a process for him, he saw me as his daughter and affectionately called me, "Poo."

Being at home gave us much more time to spend together since neither of us were working. I could talk to him about anything. He would sit in his recliner with his fingers intertwined listening attentively as I babbled on and on about this or that. He never judged, criticized, or dismissed my feelings as unimportant. And when I was done, he would lean back with this serious look on his face as if he had been in deep thought while I was talking. He started with, "Well..." (followed by some great words of wisdom. He spoke slowly and I listened with this smile on my face because I was just happy that he cared. He was one of the wisest men I knew. Then came the best part, his wonderful hugs which made me feel like whatever earth-shattering thing I was going through at the moment was going to be just fine. He easily became the most important man in my life. He loved and accepted me without me ever asking. Before I even realized what was happening that hole, the emptiness that had been gnawing at me for years was starting to fill to overflow. God gave me everything I wanted and all I had lost wrapped up in this angel on earth. And just when I thought I couldn't possibly love him anymore than I already did, he was gone.

It has been almost two years since we lost Pops; I can still remember that night just like it was last night. I was jerked out of deep thought by mothers' hysterical screams. "Help me, please help me. My husband won't wake up!" I jumped out of bed and ran to their bedroom on the other end of the house. There he was lying there with his eyes slightly opened, unresponsive. I froze, just for a second. I began CPR while my baby called the paramedics. All the while, my mother was running around frantically trying to get herself together to ride with Pops to the hospital. I had never done CPR on a person before and I was afraid that I wasn't doing it right. I prayed a selfish prayer repeatedly as I continued compressions and breaths. "Please don't leave me; please don't leave me!" I don't know how much time passed before the paramedics arrived, but it seemed like an eternity. They came and took over. They worked on him a long time. My uncle, who happens to be a pastor had arrived and began praying as we all stood by watching helplessly. The feeling of dread came over me and an unfamiliar ache filled my heart that resulted in this indescribable sinking feeling. I just couldn't shake it no matter how hard I prayed.

My daughters and I rode in silence as I offered up internal pleas to God to please not take away the man I had grown to love so much, my Pops. He was the father that I stopped hoping for. He was everything I ever wanted and then some. He was the only Papa my girls had ever known. The relationship they shared was so unique and beautiful. He loved them so much and they loved him even more. I couldn't imagine what losing him would do to us, especially my mother. How many times had she told us and anyone who would listen how he had changed her life, made her better, and was the answer to the deepest desires of her heart? He was the one true love of her life. At one point the ambulance shot passed us and the pain in my heart quickly spread throughout my entire body. Grief, heart-wrenching, soul-shaking, earth-shattering sorrow because I knew, even though I wouldn't permit myself to think nor believe it, he was already gone. We sat in the hospital room, the girls, cousins, and pastor uncle waiting for my mother or step sister to emerge from the back to tell us what I desperately wanted to be wrong about. I never wanted to be more wrong in my entire life. After what seemed like hours, my mother walked through the doors. Her face said it all but I needed to hear her say the words that I was dreading to hear. She did and we all broke! But I had to see him for myself; I refused to believe it until I saw him. Thinking back on it now, I wish I hadn't done that. My mind and heart were in agreement; neither could process what was happening. But it was real. My Pops was gone. Somehow, I managed to kiss him on the forehead and whisper, "I love you so very much, forever." I stood for a moment expecting a miracle, begging God, "Please let this be a dream. Please God, please let him wake up." I wanted that so badly, not just for me, but for my mother, my step siblings, my girls, and everyone else who loved him.

  Losing him has been one of the most devastating losses in my life. I think of him with every passing day. The very thought of him reignites that familiar ache from almost two years ago. Sometime I relive that night in my dreams. I often wonder was there anything I could have done differently. I feel a tremendous sense of guilt. There's always that nagging thought of if I had done just one thing differently, he may still be here. Then, I think of Pops on the day we said our final goodbyes. He had the most peaceful smile on his face. I had never seen anything like it before. He was actually smiling! It was like he knew something that the rest of didn't, a secret between him and God. It's that smile that brings peace to my heart. That sweet, sweet smile that reminds me that although I miss him terribly, he is with me always. I am so grateful that his life touched mine. He opened his heart and made a space for a wounded little girl who just wanted a father. I am truly blessed to be loved by him.

Daddy Teddy

As I looked down at him lying in the casket, I prayed for him to open his eyes and smile at me, but he didn't. This just couldn't be real! I couldn't believe this was happening. I tried to wrap my mind around how we got to this moment. I stared at him as tears poured down my cheeks. There was no coming back from this. It was final, over, this was the end for us. How could he be gone? How could he leave me? What was I going to do without him now? He was my daddy, the only daddy I had ever known. He was the one who acknowledged me as his own even though I wasn't. He was all I had left, the only one who wanted to be my daddy. My broken heart was flooded with pain, guilt, sorrow, and regret, so much regret. I wasn't prepared to say goodbye to the possibility of what could have been if only we had more time. I leaned over, kissed him goodbye, and said, "I love you daddy. I'm so very sorry daddy. Please forgive me." I couldn't stop the tears from falling.

You're probably confused right about now considering what I wrote previously concerning him. Everything I wrote was true from my experience of him at the time. However, there is another point of view to be considered, Teddy's. And I had no clue just how different those points of view were until after he was gone. According to everyone I spoke to after his death, he loved me with all his heart. I meant the world to him and he talked about me all the time. Every time he ran into someone who knew me, he would ask about his "PooPoo." He would tell anyone who would listen that I was his baby, he was proud of me, and how much he loved me. There were countless people coming to me and telling me the same thing repeatedly. One of the most extraordinary things I heard was from his wife. She had no idea that I wasn't his biological daughter because he never used the word step-daughter. It was an overwhelming feeling of happiness to know that he loved me so much yet, it hurt to not have heard it from him. And now I never would.

Teddy and I had a complicated relationship over the years. I loved him very much but I kept my distance from him, rather he kept his distance from me. I never knew where he was or who he was with. I ran into him from time to time and we exchanged numbers. We talked for several days in a row and then he disappeared. Either he wouldn't answer when I called or his phone was disconnected. I would see him out somewhere again and we started the pattern over again, ending with the same results as before. Soon enough I would see him but I wouldn't engage in the process anymore. I grew tired of him disappearing on me. I got tired of him telling me he was coming but never showed up. I got tired of him making promises to me that he always broke. It was always one well-intentioned lie after another and I just couldn't deal with it. Rejection from one father was enough to deal with; I just couldn't handle it from the man who chose to be my father. I had gotten to the point that I refused to keep putting myself in the position to get hurt by him. So, I just talked to him whenever he called or saw him whenever he showed up.

    Daddy started having health issues a few years ago. He was in and out of the hospital a lot. I made it a point to be there whenever he let me know he was there. He got married somewhere along the way and there were times he was in the hospital and I knew nothing about it. I missed out on a lot that was going on with him. And when we talked, he wasn't always truthful about what was really going on. Sometimes he was in the hospital because of his drinking; other times it was his heart. One time he told me he had cancer. So, I didn't know how serious it was. I probably could have done more, but I didn't know what to do. I checked in with my auntie to see if she had heard from him; sometimes she had and other times she hadn't. I went off the assumption that he was doing well since no one had heard any different. No news was good news as far as I was concerned. One day he stopped by my mother's house to see me. We argued. I was angry with him because I hadn't heard from him or seen him in a long time. He brushed off my anger with his beautiful smile. He gave me his new number and asked me to call him, but my anger wouldn't let me. That was the last time I saw him.

I spent a lot of time thinking of him in the days leading up to the funeral. This is the story that played in my mind. Here is the man who takes on another man's daughter as his own. He loves her the best way he knows how at the time. He never tells her how much she means to him. As a child, she starves for his love and attention not realizing how much he truly loves her. Time passes and resentment sets in because she feels he is obligated to love her in a way that her biological father never did, but he didn't. He loves her his way, which isn't good enough for her. More time passes and space comes between them. Lies and broken promises only confirm what she was already believes, "He doesn't love me." He tries to do better but fails most times because he's fighting his own demons. It doesn't matter because the daughter only sees her own pain. She doesn't consider that this man didn't have to choose to be her father; he didn't have to love her at all but he did his best. Although his best wasn't good enough for her, it's all he had. Could he have tried harder? Yes! Could she have tried harder? Yes! But then he dies and there is no more time left. She's heartbroken over what could have been and all the time she wasted in between. All she has left is the tremendous love he had for her that she never knew of until after he was gone.

Losing him was overwhelming for me. I cry at the very thought of him and I think of him every day. I'm filled with incredible guilt from the last time I saw him. I feel guilty that I didn't do more to strengthen our relationship. I held him to an impossible standard and I never gave him the benefit of the doubt. I stopped believing in him when he was all I had to believe in. I didn't take into consideration all the factors in his life that made him to be who he was. I didn't think about how hard it must have been for him to love another man's child as his own. As a child I needed more, expected more, deserved more and it was his responsibility to be the best father he could be. And he didn't. But when I became an adult there was an opportunity to take what I was given and build on it. I should have tried harder to be better myself and set a new level of expectation, one that he may have been capable of meeting. Now I have nothing left to build on. We can't get another chance because he is gone. I miss what I didn't know I had. I miss what we could have had. And it hurts to think that he has left this world not knowing how much I truly loved him.

Liquinita

I can't say that it was any one thing that started me on this journey of self-exploration. It was a combination of many things, a lifetime of emotionally-based decisions that led to even more destructive choices. There have been way too many mistakes to count, fueled by the never-ending desire to belong to someone. I just wanted to be wanted and completely ignored how much I truly was wanted. My mother wanted me, more than anyone else ever has. She sacrificed her life for me. She did the very best she could to ensure I had everything I needed, all I wanted, and made sure I was happy. No one on earth loves me as much as she does. Her love has been an overwhelming, sometimes smothering, but always constant unconditional force in my life. I'm so grateful to have it and I don't know who I would be without her. It was her love that taught me how to love. But still, there was always something missing. Something she couldn't provide no matter how hard she tried. And as much as I loved my amazing daughters and are loved by them, still, there was something missing. Relationships began and ended, friends came, went, and stayed, yet something was still missing. I was sure that missing part of me was found in my father. In my mind, he held the key to it all. If only he was there, everything would be different. I wouldn't have gone through any of the life experiences I had. If he was there, I would be happy because his love and acceptance was the key to it all.

Maybe I was wrong.

At some point a very long time ago, I disappeared. I felt like the me that I was becoming, even as a little girl, wasn't the me that was accepted. Although I was surrounded by love from the women in my life, I didn't feel it anywhere else. I got the distinct impression that I wasn't good enough. I didn't fit in, so I tried to make myself fit however I had to. I let myself go. The older I became the more I gave myself away. My values, beliefs and everything that made me who I was, I just let them all go. So much that I put myself in the position to be raped by someone who I just wanted to accept me as good enough. It still hurts to even say the word "rape." He stole a piece of my soul that day. It changed me forever. I gave myself away over and over again to any man that would take me until there was no more of me left. And now, when I look back on it all, none of it filled the missing part. I desperately needed to find out who I was, apart from being my mother's daughter, Alexis and Alysha's mother or somebody's someone. The roles I played, the mask I wore, the conforming and molding into someone that someone else wanted me to be left no room for me. The absence of self-worth, self-love and security in who I am left a gaping hole that needed to be filled up with me.

It's been a painful but enlightening process as I've peeled back the layers of this person that I had become, separating the parts that are purely me and those that I have allowed to be thrust upon me. Learning the parts of me that are real and genuine versus those that I have created to satisfy. The discovery of what's important to me versus what's important to someone else, things and people that I should release and those that I should hold tightly to or just simply what I really like or what I don't. I have learned to be unapologetically Liquinita. It's okay if I'd rather wear sneakers instead of heels, jeans instead of dresses, or braids instead of permed hair. It's perfectly fine if I'd rather eat a cheeseburger than a salad, or stay in and watch a movie versus going out to a club. It's alright if I'm not surrounded by a large group of friends, my faithful few are the best I could ever have. I don't have to lie to fit in. I don't have to make people like me, either they do or they don't. And it's absolutely fine if there isn't a man by my side to validate me or in my bed to make me feel loved.

I won't lie and say it's been easy, because it hasn't been. I had grown accustomed to having someone in my life to validate me and make me feel good about myself. Actually, Granny had always drilled in me to keep an "ace in the hole," which for her, basically meant to always have a backup guy. You know that someone you call when there is no one else to call. And truthfully, there was usually always *someone* I could reach back to if I so chose. But at this point in my life there is no one, absolutely no one. Just more proof that God is working behind the scenes. See, one day when I was extremely frustrated, I said a simple prayer that went something like this, "Father please take away every man in my life that I have connected my heart, soul, or body to that You don't want to be in my life." And poof, there was no one left. No one! WARNING, DON'T ASK GOD FOR SOMETHING UNLESS YOU'RE PREPARED TO RECEIVE IT! There are days when loneliness kicks in and all I want is a man to crawl up under. On those days, I regret saying that prayer, but it was necessary. Because what I desire can't be found with someone inside of me. I know, it took long enough to figure that one out.

Every once in awhile, I still struggle with being comfortable in my own skin. I often stare at myself in the mirror searching for glimpses of someone I recognize. I'm not always happy with the reflection staring back at me. I can't honestly say that I'm beautiful because I don't feel that I am. Sometimes I search for traces of my mother in my face but I can't see her there. She has been the symbol for beauty in my life, all my life. For years, I have been compared to her beauty and all I ever wanted was to come close to it. I will shamefully admit that there were times in my life that I was jealous of her and the attention her beauty drew to her. I wanted that same attention. To me that attention meant acceptance, and that's what I longed for. My mother reminded me of this one time we were in the mall together and some guy came up to her and complimented her on how beautiful she was. She flashed her beautiful smile that she's so famous for and politely said, "Thank you," without giving it any thought at all. Instead of feeling proud; I felt pure envy. It must've shown on my face because my mother quickly reassured me, "You're beautiful too baby, just like me." So, I decided to put it to the test. I went and sat on a bench in the center of the mall and waited for a guy to come and talk to me, but no one ever came. For me that only solidified what I already knew; I didn't look like my mother, therefore I wasn't beautiful.

Other times I searched for traces of my father in my reflection, but I couldn't find him either. Although I have been told all my life that I look just like him. Truth is I have never had the chance to be close enough to him to determine if that's true or not. That makes me sad, sadder than I care to admit. I've seen pictures of him and zoomed in on his face. I have spent hours staring into that face trying to find just a glimpse of myself there but I can't. Sad thing is, I want to. If I could just see some resemblance of him in me that means I have a part of him even though he wanted no part of me. It shouldn't still matter after all this time, after all the hurt, but it does. And again, I feel if I can't find him in my face then I am not beautiful. Seeing him there in my face somehow equates to me being beautiful, at least in my mind. And maybe if he sees that I am beautiful because of him, then maybe he can accept me as his own. Yea, I know it all sounds crazy right? But that's how desperately I want to be connected to him. Then that nagging question resurfaces, the one that's lived in the back of my mind forever, why doesn't my father want me? In those moments, my heart breaks knowing that there's a huge possibility that he never will. And in an instant, that hurt turns to anger. I'm angry that I have spent my entire life loving a man who doesn't even know the day I was born. Anger for all the times I have tried to be a good daughter when he could care less about being my father. Mostly, angry because I didn't ask for any of this, yet I have had to navigate my whole life around it.

And then I look in the mirror again. I take a good long look and I see me. I see that I'm still here and I don't look like what I have been through. I see that despite everything that has been taken, lost or given away that I still remain. I'm happy with the reflection I see staring back at me now. It's okay if I don't look like my mother. It's perfectly fine if I can't see my father there either. I am enough all by myself! See, I have come to understand that God knew it all from the beginning. He knew the journey I would have to take. He knew that my father wasn't coming. He knew every road I would travel. He knew every wrong turn, detour, pit stop, and the numerous times he would have to redirect me. He knew everyone I would meet along the way. He knew who I would pick up, drop off, and those who would travel with me. And He decided to always wait for me because he knew there would be times that I would leave Him behind and then double back to pick Him up again. He also knew that there would come a period in my life that I would trust Him to guide me because I had no clue where I was going. That time is now and I can't wait to see where I'll end up.

Acknowledgements

I would like to thank my Father God for placing this book within me. Thank you, God, for the courage and strength to see it through until the end. Pastor Uncle Glen Mims, thank you for speaking into my life. Thank you for prayers and personal conferences. You called out my gifts and forced me to use them; I can never repay you for that. You spoke this book into existence many times, when I wanted to quit. I have grown so much under your spiritual guidance. Thank you for seeing the best in me, calling me by my name, "Mighty Woman of God," and encouraging me to be unapologetically Liquinita.

Thank you, Dr. Sonia Cunningham Leverette of Hadassah's Crown Publishing, LLC, for accepting this book for publication. I appreciate your support and honest feedback during the process of finishing this project. I admire your passion for helping new authors birth their dreams. I look forward to working with you in the future.

Thank you, Natasha Perlotte, for agreeing to help make this dream come true. You treated my dream as if was your own. Amazing! You have been my eyes, seeing everything that I couldn't, always having my best interest at heart. I'm so blessed to have you on my team! You have done so much leg work behind the scenes of this project; I'm so grateful. More than anything, thanks for giving me my Nugget, Savannah Grace. I love you both so so so much!

Thank you, Mommy, for loving me so completely and unconditionally all the days of my life. You have seen greatness in me that I never saw in myself. You have always believed in me and been my supporter and number one fan. You sacrificed your life for mine; there's no greater love than that. I'm so blessed that God chose you for me! I love you more than words can ever express.

Alexis and Alysha, the loves of my life, thank you for always seeing the best in me. Alexis, you have been my strength, the one who has challenged me to grow beyond my disability. You are the only person in my life who know exactly what it feels to live this life as a legally blind individual. Alysha, my baby, thanks for taking such good care of me since you were able to walk. You have always tried to make sure my heart was safe when it was my job to protect yours. You see past my limitations to my greatness. Thank you both for forcing me to be the best version of myself and never giving up on me. Thanks for the faith in me that I could write a book and pushing me to get it done. I am grateful for our beautiful relationship and the unbreakable bond that we share. I love you both with every beat of my heart.

Auntie Stella and Uncle Westley, I love you both very much! Auntie, you are strength and have insisted that I be strong as well. You have never allowed me to use my disability as an excuse for anything. You held me to a standard of excellence in every area of my life. You have taken care of me, then my girls, always making sure we have everything we needed. Thanks for believing that I can do great things! I hope I have made you proud. Uncle Wes, thanks for being one of the most important men in my life. Your love has been a blanket of warmth and consistency since you came into our family. Thanks for including me as one of your own! I will always be your Pookie!

Mary Callaham, my mama and the matriarch of our family, you are my heart. Thank you for your love and support. Thank you for helping me raise my beautiful babies. I think I would have gone insane if you weren't there to help me. I cherish our special bond and I'm grateful for everything you do. I love you with my whole heart!

Kenya Calhoun, thank you for your love and support. Thank you for putting up with all my mood swings and emotional breakdowns. Thanks for letting me be my complicated self with no judgements. No one has pushed me during the project more than you. I'm so blessed to have our divine connection, and your prayers have upheld me through so many life trials. You are truly the bestest. best friend of all the best friends in the entire universe. I love me some you!

Kimberly Bland, thank you for ALWAYS seeing past my disability and treating me as an equal. You have made yourself available to the girls and me whenever we've needed you. I can't think of a time that I needed something from you that you didn't come through for me. You have been my nurse, driver and dearest and cherished friend. I can't imagine my life without you there. I love you so much!

LaShanda Blair, thanks for taking the time to do my hair for the headshot photos. I asked for something a bit funky and you did exactly that. No one makes me laugh like you do. Your silly sense of humor and generous heart are just a couple of the reasons I keep you around. LOL! I value your place in my life and I'm grateful for your presence. Love ya sisterly!

Auntie Gloria Bell, our family photographer, thanks for being an encouraging and supportive part of my life. Thanks for the beautiful pictures. You sure do know how to make a girl look good! You are absolutely the best and I love you!

To my Sugaface, April Coley, thanks for being my counselor for free. Lol! Thanks for always being there for me and helping take care of my girls. Thanks for holding me up when my world seemed to be crashing down around me. Thanks for fighting my battles when I couldn't. Your love and encouragement have been constant and I'm blessed to have you. I am so extremely proud of the woman you have become. You're more than a cousin; you're my sister. I love you past the moon!

My Redd, LaTonya Owings, my sista/cousin, thanks for taking care of my eyes. You make sure I have the right glasses to see clearly. If it weren't for you getting the wonderful pair I have now, I wouldn't have been able to see to even write this book. You are an everyday part of my life. So blessed that Auntie trusted me with you. Taking care of you was practice for me being a mother to my babies. And maybe my

example played a part of you being an amazing mother to yours. Love you past the moon!

About the Author

Liquinita L. Callaham was born in Greenwood, SC and raised in McCormick, SC. Jesus Christ found her at a very young age, and she credits Him for her physical and emotional healing, as well as giving her life meaning and purpose. She became legally blind at 19 and faced various health issues throughout the years. Despite her challenges, she earned a Bachelor's Degree in Psychology from Converse College in 2014.  She has a great love for children, and her passion is helping children and young adults with blindness and visual disabilities. Ms. Callaham has worked with the South Carolina School for the Deaf and Blind and the South Carolina Commission for the Blind. She is also a member of the Healthy Eyes Foundation for the Blind of South Carolina. She notes the single most important job she's ever had and the greatest accomplishment of her life as being mother to her extraordinary daughters, Alexis and Alysha.

Ms. Callaham says of her daughters, "I'm so blessed that God chose and trusted me with being their mother. They are my happy place, the joys of my life and the greatest love I have ever known!" **She can be contacted for book signings, appearances and bulk sales at llcallaham@yahoo.com.**

For information about publishing opportunities, visit our website or email HadassahsCrown@gmail.com.

www.ingramcontent.com/pod-product-compliance
Lightning Source LLC
Chambersburg PA
CBHW070537010526
44118CB00012B/1149